People, Places,
Checkmates

PEOPLE, PLACES, CHECKMATES

Teaching Social Studies with Chess

Alexey W. Root

A Teacher Ideas Press Book

LIBRARIES UNLIMITED

AN IMPRINT OF ABC-CLIO, LLC
Santa Barbara, California • Denver, Colorado • Oxford, England

Library of Congress Cataloging-in-Publication Data

Root, Alexey W.
  People, places, checkmates : teaching social studies with chess / Alexey W. Root.
     p. cm.
   "A Teacher Ideas Press Book."
   Includes bibliographical references and index.
    ISBN 978-1-59158-850-4 (alk. paper)—ISBN 978-1-59158-852-8 (ebook)
   1. Social sciences—Study and teaching (Elementary)—United States.   2. Social sciences—Study and teaching (Secondary)—United States.   3. Chess—Study and teaching (Elementary)
4. Chess—Study and teaching (Middle school)   I. Title.
   LB1584.R66   2010
   372.83'044—dc22   2009051265

ISBN: 978-1-59158-850-4
EISBN: 978-1-59158-852-8

14   13   12   11   10   1   2   3   4   5

This book is also available on the World Wide Web as an eBook.
Visit www.abc-clio.com for details.

Libraries Unlimited
An Imprint of ABC-CLIO, LLC

ABC-CLIO, LLC
130 Cremona Drive, P.O. Box 1911
Santa Barbara, California 93116-1911

This book is printed on acid-free paper ∞

Manufactured in the United States of America

For Diane Savereide,
Six-time U.S. women's chess champion and my role model

CONTENTS

Chapter 1

INTRODUCTION

National Council for the Social Studies

This book teaches social studies for grades four through eight in 15 lesson plans. Each plan may be taught in 40 minutes or less. Plans highlight chess in civics, economics, history, the humanities, geography, government, political science, psychology, and technology. Each plan focuses on one National Council for the Social Studies (NCSS) theme, as shown in Figure 1.1. Every plan lists its objectives, NCSS theme, materials and sources, procedure, and evaluation. Plans do not require knowledge of the rules of chess.

An optional chess exercise accompanies each plan. To complete the exercises, students must know the rules of chess and **algebraic notation.** These chess basics are explained in chapter 5. Additionally, chess terms are in bold font when first used and are defined in the glossary. Bold font is also used for chess **moves** played in a game; **variations** are in regular font. Each chess exercise includes teacher background, procedure and materials, expected time, and evaluation.

Some exercises take 10 minutes; others up to 25 minutes. For a 40–50-minute class period, you might teach the plan on the first day. Then you can either skip the exercise or save it for another time. Some exercises are suitable for homework. For a class period of more than 50 minutes, the chess exercise might serve as prelesson warm-up or be given to students who finish the lesson plan quickly.

Table showing the connection of lesson plans in *People, Places, Checkmates* to the 10 themes of the National Council for the Social Studies (Schneider, 1994, pp. 21–30).

Lesson Plan	NCSS Thematic Strand
1. Timelines	II. Time, Continuity, & Change. Social studies programs should include experiences that provide for the study of the ways human beings view themselves in and over time.
2. Maps	III. People, Places, & Environments. Social studies programs should include experiences that provide for the study of people, places, and environments.
3. Silk Road	VII. Production, Distribution, & Consumption. Social studies programs should include experiences that provide for the study of how people organize for the production, distribution, and consumption of goods and services.
4. Legends around the World	IX. Global Connections. Social studies programs should include experiences that provide for the study of global connections and interdependence.
5. Write a Legend	IV. Individual Development & Identity. Social studies programs should include experiences that provide for the study of individual development and identity.
6. Rule Changes	VIII. Science, Technology, & Society. Social studies programs should include experiences that provide for the study of relationships among science, technology, and society.
7. Noble Charades	V. Individuals, Groups, & Institutions. Social studies programs should include experiences that provide for the study of interactions among individuals, groups, and institutions.
8. Chess Legend of Columbus	II. Time, Continuity, & Change. Social studies programs should include experiences that provide for the study of the ways human beings view themselves in and over time.
9. The Turk, Automaton Chess Player	VIII. Science, Technology, & Society. Social studies programs should include experiences that provide for the study of relationships among science, technology, and society.
10. Federal Sets	VI. Power, Authority, & Governance. Social studies programs should include experiences that provide for the study of how people create and change structures of power, authority, and governance.
11. Benjamin Franklin	I. Culture. Social studies programs should include experiences that provide for the study of culture and cultural diversity.
12. Famous Chess Players	IV. Individual Development & Identity. Social studies programs should include experiences that provide for the study of individual development and identity.
13. Chess Philanthropy	IX. Global Connections. Social studies programs should include experiences that provide for the study of global connections and interdependence.
14. Chess Scholarships	V. Individuals, Groups, & Institutions. Social studies programs should include experiences that provide for the study of interactions among individuals, groups, and institutions.
15. Immigration	X. Civic Ideals & Practices. Social studies programs should include experiences that provide for the study of the ideals, principles, and practices of citizenship in a democratic republic.

Figure 1.1.
Themes from the National Council for the Social Studies (NCSS).

Lesson Plan Overview

Chapter 1 introduces chapters 2–5. It also chronicles the development of the lesson plans. In chapter 2, students study the premodern chess era (450–1475). Chess began in India. Students create a timeline of the evolution of chess and other games. Students map the dissemination of chess through the expansion of the Islamic empire. Students dramatize how traders over the Silk Road may have modified chess. Students read chess legends from several cultures. Students write their own chess legends.

As chapter 3 explains, modern chess began in 1475, after chess arrived in Western Europe. One change was that the vizier, which had limited movement, was replaced by an agile **queen.** Students compare the premodern, slow-paced game of chess to modern chess. Students dramatize the skills, which included chess, of noblemen and noblewomen. Students respond to historical accounts about the recall of Columbus, perhaps because of a chess game. Students debate whether the Turk Chess **Automaton** was a good use of technology. Students design **set**s of federal leaders.

In chapter 4, students connect chess and citizenship. Students apply *The Morals of Chess* by Benjamin Franklin. Students recognize famous chess players. Students learn about chess philanthropy by **Grandmaster (GM)** Yury Shulman's organization "Chess Without Borders." Students understand the criteria for college chess scholarships. Students debate participation guidelines for chess-playing immigrants to the United States.

Chapter 5 has the rules of chess and how to read and write algebraic notation. From chapter 5, an educator could create his or her own "how to play chess" lessons. Or the educator might teach chess from my previous three books (Root, 2006; Root, 2008b; and Root, 2009b). Root (2009b, Appendix B) tells how to run **ladder** games and **tournament**s, both of which are referred to in this present book. Appendix A has an answer key for the lesson plans and exercises from chapters 2–4, and for one worksheet from chapter 5. Appendix B contains annotated references and photo credits. Appendix C lists higher education institutions with chess programs.

Over the past 30 years, I have thought about the connections between chess and history. I was a history major at the University of Puget Sound; a world history, U.S. history, and English teacher at Bakersfield High School; and a graduate student researcher at the National Center for History in the Schools at the University of California, Los Angeles. During those same years, I was also a chess player and a chess teacher. At present, for two courses in the **Chess in Education Certificate Online** program, I include history books by Shenk (2006) and Yalom (2004).

In the summer of 2008, I prepared a proposal for this book. My editor, Sharon Coatney, suggested the NCSS Curriculum Standards. After reading those standards (Schneider, 1994), I wrote social studies plans and accompanying chess exercises. In the fall of 2008, a draft of new NCSS Curriculum Standards was posted on the NCSS Web site. I also matched my lesson plans to that prepublication draft.

Organization of Chess Classes

In the summers of 2008 and 2009, at the MOSAIC (Marvelous Opportunities Scheduled as Individual Courses) summer enrichment organized by the Coppell Gifted Association (http://www.coppellgifted.org), I tested these social studies plans and chess exercises. MOSAIC chess courses ran from 9 A.M. to noon Monday through Friday and enrolled students entering grades four through eight in the fall. Students did not have to be gifted to attend MOSAIC courses. Some students came to the MOSAIC chess courses as **beginners.**

For the 2008–2009 school year, I volunteered three times a week as a chess instructor during advisory period (generally called simply advisory) at Strickland Middle School (SMS). Root (2009a) explains the history, rationale, and research behind SMS enrichment advisories. Enrichment advisory classes at SMS in 2008–2009 were for students who:

1. Scored 2200 or higher on all sections of the Texas Assessment of Knowledge and Skills (TAKS) on the last TAKS administered. On the TAKS, 2100 is the passing standard, and a commended performance is 2400 or higher, and
2. Maintained passing grades. If a student had a failing grade (less than 70), on a 3-week progress report or a 6-week report card, then that student was reassigned to study hall until his or her grades improved to passing (after three such assignments to study hall, the student was not allowed to return to his or her enrichment advisory), and
3. Were not already in an audition-only advisory such as jazz band, show choir, or orchestra.

During an assembly on September 10, 2008, about 330 eligible students chose from advisory options offered by 13 teachers. Advisory options included sixth-grade sports, seventh- and eighth-grade sports, art, chess, computer, handbells, library, puzzles and games, Rachel's Challenge, Spanish, and theater. For those students, Mondays and Wednesdays of advisory were now study skills and character education. Tuesdays, Thursdays, and Fridays were devoted to each student's chosen enrichment. Most students got their first choice of advisory, though some got their second or third choices instead.

On September 15, 19 boys and 1 girl joined me and seventh-grade math teacher Mr. Steve McClanahan, who taught the advisory on Mondays and Wednesdays. Because his classroom was small, we moved computers to make space for chess**board**s. During the fall semester, attendance dipped to 11 during one 3-week period and rebounded to 20 during another. For the spring semester, chess advisory usually had 20 students.

The first 10 minutes were for the pledges to the U.S. and Texas flags, a moment of silence, announcements over the public address system, and taking roll. If chess supplies were needed that day, another 5 minutes were for getting out, and putting away, those supplies. Therefore, each 40-minute advisory period had about 25 to 30 minutes of teaching time. Sometimes special events such as pep rallies and awards assemblies pre-empted advisory. Thus, between the first day of chess advisory and the December holiday break, I taught about 15 hours. From January through May I taught about 20 hours.

On the first chess day of a week, for September and most of October, I taught lesson plans and activities from Root (2006) or Root (2008b). I sometimes used a **demonstration board.** The cost for a 36-inch-square demonstration board with pieces, shown in Figure 1.2, is around $30 (including shipping) from American Chess Equipment (http://www. amchesseq.com).

On the second chess day per week, I paired the 8 returning, **intermediate** chess students (trainers) with the 12 students new to chess advisory (trainees). Students enjoyed the analogy of a Pokémon trainer preparing a Pokémon for battle. Each trainer used the chart in Figure 1.3 to track his or her trainee's progress. Abbreviations on Figure 1.3 are: P is for **pawn,** R is for **rook,** B is for **bishop,** N is for **knight,** Q is for queen, K is for **king,** + means **check,** e.p. is for **en passant,** and # means **checkmate.** Thus K&2R# means a king and two rooks check-mating a lone king. To guide their teaching of chess rules, **stalemate**s, **tactics,** and basic checkmates, trainers used the book that they and their colleagues wrote the previous year. That book is chapter 5 of Root (2009b). After October 29, when all students began notating their lad-der games, trainer–trainee days also included **post mortem**s of ladder games.

My guidelines for post mortems were adapted from my **annotation** guidelines of the previous chess advisory year (Root, 2009b, chapter 4). As with the annotation guidelines, post-mortem guidelines addressed the student(s) whose game was being analyzed. But post mortems also involved students who had not played the game under scrutiny. Those outside students may not be able to answer why a move was played, but can still explain why a move was poor or good. I additionally directed those outside students to give three compliments for every one criticism, so as not to spoil the mood of the game's player or players (van Wijgerden, 2008, p. 48).

Therefore, the following post-mortem guidelines apply to everyone participating in the post mortem:

Figure 1.2.
Demonstration board.

TRAINER–TRAINEE RESPONSIBILITIES.

TRAINEE MUST KEEP THIS CHART IN HIS OR HER FOLDER.

Name of Trainer:

Name of Trainee:

Required:

1. Trainer must have trainee read and answer questions in *one Chess Book section per training day*. Sections include topics such as pawn, rook, check, Sicilian, and so forth.

2. Trainer must play out on a chess set and board, with the trainee, the section's chess exercise.

3. Trainer needs to date (month/day) the completion of the section in the chart, with month on top and day below. September 20th completion of the Pawn section would be written as:

P
9
20

P	R	B	Q	K	+	K&2R#	K&Q#	K&R#	Stalemate	N	e.p.	Promotion	Castle	Scholar's	Sicilian

Extra:

4. If numbers 1–3 above have been completed, and there are notated ladder games to review, the trainer and trainees should analyze those together (post mortems). For how to conduct a post mortem see Figure A.13.

5. If there is still time left in class, trainer and trainee may play a chess game, practice a chess drill, or read chess books. If the trainer has more than one trainee, trainer could have the trainees play against each other. Trainer should write on the back of this page what extra things this trainee has learned, and date those items, for example: Trainee learned what a fork was on 10/10, or Trainee learned the Ruy Lopez opening on 11/22.

Figure 1.3.
Chart for trainers and trainees.

From *People, Places, Checkmates: Teaching Social Studies with Chess* by Alexey W. Root. Santa Barbara, CA: Libraries Unlimited. Copyright © 2010.

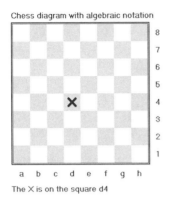

Chess diagram with algebraic notation

The X is on the square d4

Figure 1.4.
Algebraic square naming.

1. Tell if your **opening** followed the **ABCD** principles.
2. Tell when you played a good move and why it was good. Usually, good moves for one's side won **material** or **points, develop**ed **pieces,** or improved king safety.
3. Tell why you played a poor move and why it was poor. Poor moves for one's side lost material, left pieces undeveloped on the back rank, or put the king in danger.
4. Tell how material was lost or won, such as by a **pin,** a **skewer,** a **fork,** a **discovered check,** or by having left a **chessman en prise.**

Chess Equipment

Figure 1.5.
Students using standard chess equipment.

Figure 1.6.
Setting a chess clock.

Trainers and trainees used boards and sets. Boards had algebraic notation marked around the outside borders. In algebraic notation, **files** are labeled a–h, and **ranks** are labeled 1–8. As shown in the **diagram** in Figure 1.4, a square is described file-first, followed by rank. Boards with notation are often sold with a **Staunton** set. To meet tournament and teaching standards, yet keep costs low, one can match a solid-plastic set (with a king that measures 3.75 inches in height) with a 20-inch vinyl board. If ordered in quantity, the cost for each board and set combination works out to about $6. In Figure 1.5, an 11- and a 10-year-old study a **position** on such a set and board. In this book, boards and sets refer to boards with notation on their borders and to Staunton sets. As mentioned in *Science, Math, Checkmate* (Root, 2008b, pp. 6–7), free boards and sets are available for qualified schools from the U.S. Chess Trust (http://www.uschesstrust.org/WP/).

On the third chess day of a week, my chess advisory students played a ladder game. Starting on October 29, 2008, students used notebook paper as **score sheet**s and occasionally used **clocks.** My son William, a seventh grader in the SMS chess advisory, is shown setting a chess clock for 30 minutes per side in Figure 1.6.

Students quickly learned chess basics, from their trainer and from me. By late October, all students were familiar with chess

Basic Checkmates Testing. Results from fall 2007 are in italics; results from December 2008 and January 2009 are listed in regular font. For columns 2–7 across the top of the form, white chessmen are listed first, then "vs.", then black chessmen. I recorded the best result for each year (2007, 2008, and 2009). Best result means fewest moves on the toughest checkmate attempted. The easier mates are to the left of the chart, and the tougher mates are to the right. This particular chart shows the number of moves (white–black move pairs), after the last pawn move, to checkmate for 11 of my 20 chess advisory students. White moves first.

1	2	3	4	5	6	7
Name	Kh1 & Qa1 vs. Kd5	Kh1 & Ra1 vs. Kd5	Ke3 & Pe2 (promote to Q) vs. Kd5	Ke3 & Pe2 (promote to R) vs. Kd5	Ke1 & 2Bs (c1, f1) vs. Kd5	Ke1 & Bc1& Ng1 vs. Kd5
Andrew A.			*2007, 19 moves*; 2008, 18 moves; 2009, 15 moves			
Jared				*2007, 27 moves*; 2008, 16 moves		
Spencer	2009, 15 moves					
Luis			*2007, 14 moves*	2009, 15 moves		
Andrew K.			2009, 11 moves			
Matthew M.			2008, 9 moves	*2007, 13 moves*		
William					*2007, 28 moves*	2009, 32 moves
Matthew S.			*2007, 24 moves*; 2009, 11 moves			
Kyler			2009, 10 moves			
Jacob			2009, 16 moves	2009, 33 moves		
Andrew G.			2009, 9 moves			

Figure 1.7.
Students' best results on basic checkmates.

From *People, Places, Checkmates: Teaching Social Studies with Chess* by Alexey W. Root. Santa Barbara, CA: Libraries Unlimited. Copyright © 2010.

Basic Checkmates Testing. For columns 2–7 across the top of the form, white chessmen are listed first, then "vs.", then black chessmen. Count moves (white–black move pairs) from after the last pawn move (a promotion) until checkmate for columns 4 and 5. The easier mates are to the left of the chart, and the tougher mates are to the right. White moves first.

1	2	3	4	5	6	7
Name	Kh1 & Qa1 vs. Kd5	Kh1 & Ra1 vs. Kd5	Ke3 & Pe2 (promote to Q) vs. Kd5	Ke3 & Pe2 (promote to R) vs. Kd5	Ke1 & 2Bs (c1, f1) vs. Kd5	Ke1 & Bc1& Ng1 vs. Kd5

Figure 1.8.
Form for recording students' basic checkmate results.

From *People, Places, Checkmates: Teaching Social Studies with Chess* by Alexey W. Root. Santa Barbara, CA: Libraries Unlimited. Copyright © 2010.

To: Parents of chess advisory students

From: Alexey Root <aroot@utdallas.edu>

During the three days a week of chess advisory (1–3 below), students:

1. Work with each other to improve at chess (trainer–trainee day).

2. Play a ladder game.

3. Learn from my instruction on chess topics. I was the 1989 U.S. Women's Chess Champion and am the volunteer chess teacher for Strickland.

In addition to chess instruction, I will be teaching 15 different social studies topics on my instructional day each week. Topics this fall include:

1. Beginning of chess in India about 1,500 years ago.

2. Creating a timeline comparing the invention date of chess to the debuts of other games.

3. Mapping the dissemination of chess through the expansion of the Islamic empire.

4. Modification of chess rules by Silk Road traders.

5. Reading chess legends from several cultures, then students writing their own chess legends.

Based on my chess teaching, I write books, including: *Children and Chess: A Guide for Educators* (2006), *Science, Math, Checkmate: 32 Chess Activities for Inquiry and Problem Solving* (2008); and *Read, Write, Checkmate: Enrich Literacy with Chess Activities* (to be published in spring 2009; based on 2007–2008 chess advisory students' work). This academic year, I am working on my fourth book, *People, Places, Checkmates: Teaching Social Studies with Chess*. The expected publication date is the spring of 2010. The book will be based on this 2008–2009 academic year. **If you sign and return the attached release form, I will be able to include your student's work and photo(s) in this book.** If you have any questions, please email me at aroot@utdallas.edu.

For social studies-chess activities, students need to bring colored pencils. One activity is the Silk Road trading game. Please send one or more items listed in the table.

The items will be returned to you after the game:

Figure 1.9.
Parent information letter.

From *People, Places, Checkmates: Teaching Social Studies with Chess* by Alexey W. Root. Santa Barbara, CA: Libraries Unlimited. Copyright © 2010.

Goods from the West (Persia and Central Asia)	Goods from China
Glass	Silk
Gold	Bronze
Silver	Lacquer work
Gems	Ceramics
Woolen and linen fabrics	Iron
Chairs	Apricots
Vines	Oranges
Fig trees	Mulberries
Flax	Pomegranates
Jasmine	Peaches
Dates	Roses
Indian spices	Camellias
Olives	Peonies
Silver drachmas (engraved circular coins); multiple coins needed. Could substitute quarters.	Chinese coins (round coin with square hole in the middle); multiple coins needed. Could substitute hardware nuts.

Figure 1.9.
(continued).

From *People, Places, Checkmates: Teaching Social Studies with Chess* by Alexey W. Root. Santa Barbara, CA: Libraries Unlimited. Copyright © 2010.

STUDENT WORK AND PHOTO RELEASE FORM

The parent or guardian _____ of the student _____ grants to the author/photographer Dr. Alexey Root and to her assignees and licensees the absolute right and permission to use, publish, or sell the student work(s) and the photograph(s) created during Strickland MS (SMS) chess advisory (October, 2008–May, 2009), in which the student has created work or is included in photos, in any medium, throughout the world, without any restriction whatsoever as to the nature of the use or publication or as to the copy of any printed matter accompanying the photograph(s). I understand that the student work and the images may be altered and I waive the right to approve of any finished product. I understand that I do not own the copyright of the student work or the photograph(s). I certify that I am over 18 years of age and that I have the full legal right to execute this agreement.

NAME of author/photographer: Alexey Root (SMS chess teacher, aroot@utdallas.edu)

DESCRIPTION of student work: Students' written assignments about different aspects of chess. The student certifies that the work is original. Students will be identified by first name and grade level only.

DESCRIPTION of photography: Photos of students playing chess or working on chess advisory assignments. Student will be identified by first name and grade level only.

SIGNATURE of student: **DATE:**

NAME of student:

AGE of student *(if under 18 years of age)***:**

Name of Parent/Guardian

Signature of Parent/Guardian

ADDRESS of student:

_____

_____

Telephone: _____

Email address: _____

Figure 1.10.
Parent release form.

From *People, Places, Checkmates: Teaching Social Studies with Chess* by Alexey W. Root. Santa Barbara, CA: Libraries Unlimited. Copyright © 2010.

and had experience playing ladder games. In December, and on some trainer–trainee days in spring of 2009, I tested students on basic checkmates such as king and queen versus king. Some of my students' scores on the basic checkmates as of January 2009 are recorded in Figure 1.7. Figure 1.7 also includes the best result from the previous year, when available, so that students could see their progress from December 2007 to December 2008/January 2009. I counted moves from after the last pawn move. That is because, in a real chess game, one has 50 moves (white–black move pairs) after the last pawn move (or **capture** of any type) to complete a **win** before the game is declared a **draw**. Figure 1.8 is a blank version of the form to use with your students.

Starting in the last week of October until the end of May, I taught one of the 15 plans or chess exercises from chapters 2–4 on the first chess day (Tuesday) of each week. The plans did not require getting out chess sets and boards. Unless the chess exercise required very little time, or the plan teaching went surprisingly quickly, I saved the related chess exercise for the next Tuesday or for the Thursday trainer–trainee day. If the latter, before the trainers and trainees started on their usual routine, they would solve the chess exercise. In summary, the chess advisory weekly pattern was

Tuesday: For September and most of October, I taught lesson plans and activities from Root (2006) or Root (2008b). From late October until the end of May, I taught a social studies lesson or chess exercise from *People, Places, Checkmates.*

Thursday: Trainer–trainee day. This day sometimes included a chess exercise from *People, Places, Checkmates.* In December 2008 and the spring of 2009, I tested or retested students for the charts shown in Figure 1.7.

Friday: Ladder game, required to be notated after late October. If ladder games did not finish during the Friday advisory class, Mr. McClanahan allowed students to finish after his Monday and Wednesday lessons.

I include samples of SMS student work, along with MOSAIC student work, in Appendix A. I also took photos. To publish students' photos or work, adapt Figure 1.9 and Figure 1.10.

Chapter 2

THE WORLD OF CHESS

The lessons in this chapter may be taught in any order. With my SMS 2008–2009 students, I began with lesson 3. Then I taught lessons 1, 2, 4, and 5.

For lesson 1, students create a timeline of the development of chess and other games. In lesson 2, students map the dissemination of chess through the expansion of the Islamic empire. During lesson 3, students dramatize how traders over the Silk Road may have modified chess. In lesson 4, students read and analyze chess legends from several cultures. For lesson 5, students write their own chess legends.

If students will be attempting the optional chess exercises, first teach or review the rules of chess in chapter 5. Usually there is a one-to-one correspondence between lesson plans and the chess exercises. But lesson 5 has a bonus exercise, exercise 5-B.

Lesson 1: Timelines

Objectives

Students compare and contrast the longevity of chess and other popular games. Students construct timelines.

NCSS Theme

II. Time, Continuity, & Change.

Materials and Sources

A piece of blank paper or notebook paper and a pencil for each student. Optional: a ruler, crayons, and colored pencils for each student. Alternatively, have students construct the timeline using computer software.

The idea for this lesson plan came from Shenk (2006, pp. 17–18, 232–235), and Pandolfini (2007, p. 166).

Procedure

Write the following on the chalk- or dry-erase board: "Gameboy is ____ years old. Monopoly is ____ years old. Baseball is ____ years old. Backgammon is ____ years old. Chess is ____ years old." For the purposes of this timeline, backgammon and chess include identifiable predecessors of those games. After students guess, provide the correct answers. For a math challenge, write how old the game is but ask students to calculate the date of its invention. For example, fill in the blank for Gameboy with "21" because Gameboy is 21 years old as of 2010. Then ask students to calculate the invention date of Gameboy.

Write the following invention dates on the board: Gameboy (1989), Monopoly (1933), baseball (1845), and **chatrang** (about 600), "the first true version of what we now call chess" (Shenk, 2006, p. 17), nard (third century), an ancestor of backgammon, a dice and strategy game from India (Eales, 1985, pp. 25, 31). Shenk (p. 18) wrote about chess, "The game probably evolved along the famous Silk Road trading routes, which for centuries carried materials, information, and ideas." For more on the Silk Road, see lesson 3.

Add the following approximate dates for chess: possible Indian ancestor of chess (**chaturanga**, 450); first Arabic writings on chess's predecessor (**shatranj**, 850), first Scandinavian and European references to chess, including the not-yet-powerful queen (1000), and chess rules modernized (1475). Add the era of the Silk Road land trading routes, according to GeoQuest (2000) (5th century B.C.E.–10th century C.E.). Some historians think chess originated in China and moved westward. Others believe that chess traveled from India to China. In the Silk Road dramatization in lesson 3, Arabs transmitted shatranj to China around the ninth century.

Here are the invention dates for chess and the other games in list form.

- 5th century B.C.E.–10th century C.E.: Silk Road land trading routes
- 2nd to 3rd century C.E.: nard (backgammon predecessor)
- 450: chaturanga, chesslike game from India
- 600: chatrang, Persian chess predecessor
- 850: first Arabic writings about shatranj (same game as chatrang)
- 1000: chess comes to Europe and queen introduced
- 1475: modern chess rules

- 1845: baseball
- 1933: Monopoly
- 1989: Gameboy

If students are using a blank paper or notebook paper for their time-lines, tell them to turn the paper to landscape format. That is, the timeline should have the earliest date near the left of the horizontally placed page, and the most recent date near the right edge. Most notebook paper has a red line next to the three-hole side that can function as the timeline. Make sure the holes, and the line for the timeline, are closest to the bottom of the page when the notebook paper is horizontal. Write dates between the line and the hole edge of the paper, and write descriptions between the line and the far edge of the paper. Because of the vast difference between the year 500 B.C.E. (start of Silk Road trading routes) and the year 1989 (Gameboy), ask them if years, decades, centuries, or millennia would be the best choice as timeline intervals. Then, if they have not already come up with the answer themselves, advise students to use centuries. If students have blank paper, provide rulers and give suggestions for construct-ing intervals on the timeline. Draw a timeline on the board as a model.

After your instructions and modeling, each student makes a timeline. Optional: Students draw pictures of the games and the Silk Road with crayon or colored pencil. Ask students how many years chess, in some form, has lasted. Tell them that backgammon, because it uses dice, was sometimes banned. In contrast, chess was often praised for exercising the mind and for developing military strategy. Chess, too, was occasion-ally banned because of dice use (see exercise 7), representational pieces (Islamic scriptural ban on images), distracting from spiritual matters, and gambling on the results of chess. Then ask students to write, on the backs of their timelines, why they think chess is an example of historical continuity.

Evaluation

Collect paper timelines, or printouts of the computer work. An eighth grader's timeline and historical-continuity paragraph is in Appendix A. Respond to students' answers about chess and historical continuity with individual comments on the backs of their papers, or refer to students' timelines and paragraphs when introducing lessons 4 and 5.

Exercise 1: Chatrang and Shatranj

Teacher Background

To create Figure 2.1, I consulted Shenk (2006, p. 31) and Eales (1985, pp. 19, 23). From chaturanga evolved the Persian chatrang. Chatrang passed on its rules to the Arabic shatranj. Modern chess evolved from shatranj.

Directions. Fill in column 6 based on the information in columns 1–5. Except for the pawn (P), all chessmen capture in the same way that they move. The pawn is the only chessman which may not move backward. Only the knight can hop over other chessmen. The term "chessmen" refers to pieces and pawns. The term "pieces" refers to the king (K), queen (Q), rook (R), bishop (B), and knight (N). Until the year 1000, the squares of the board were separated by lines but were all the same color (no black squares).

1	2	3	4	5	6
Persia, chatrang (600)	*Arabic, shatranj (850)*	*Meaning*	*Rules of movement from shatranj*	*Modern rules for chess, Europe, 1475. Exception: Castling only became standard after 1600.*	*Name today*
Shah	Shah	King	One square in any direction. May not stay in, or move into, check. No castling.	Same as column 4, except that kings can castle once per game.	
Farzin	Firz or Firzan	Counselor or Vizier	Moves only one diagonal square at a time.	May choose, for each turn, to move either like a rook or like a bishop.	
Pil	Fil	Elephant	Jumps to second diagonal square. Never occupies first diagonal square.	Moves on unobstructed squares on a diagonal.	
Asp	Faras	Horse	Moves in a capital L: 2 squares horizontally then 1 square vertically, or 2 squares vertically and then 1 horizontally.	Same as column 4.	
Rukh	Rukh	Chariot	Moves on unobstructed files and ranks.	Column 4, plus castling.	
Pujada	Baidaq	Foot Soldier	Moves forward one unobstructed square. Promotes to Firzan on back rank.	Column 4, plus optional two-square jump on 1st move. Promotes to Q, R, B, or N.	

Figure 2.1.
Guess the chessmen.

From *People, Places, Checkmates: Teaching Social Studies with Chess* by Alexey W. Root. Santa Barbara, CA: Libraries Unlimited. Copyright © 2010.

Procedure and Materials

Pass out copies of Figure 2.1 for students to complete as an individual exercise. Students need pencils or pens. Have students save their completed copies of Figure 2.1 for use in later exercises.

Expected Time

10 minutes.

Evaluation

The answer key for Figure 2.1 is in Appendix A.

Lesson 2: Maps

Objectives

Students map the expansion of the Islamic empire during Muhammad's lifetime and in the century after Muhammad's death. Students list three areas of interaction (religion, chess, and culture/inventions) between the Muslims and the people in their conquered regions.

NCSS Theme

III. People, Places, & Environments.

Materials and Sources

Copies of Figures 2.2 and 2.3 for each student. More information and maps are in: Cohen and Douglass (2006, pp. 6, 18, 23–26), Eales (1985, pp. 24, 37), Geoquest (2000, map 8), Gover (2006, pp. 5–6 and Index), Matthew (1983, pp. 49–51), Matthews (1991, pp. 18–19), Shenk (2006, pp. 47–48), Yalom (2004, p. 6), and the Web site *1001 Inventions* (http://www.1001inventions.com). Optional: Turn Figure 2.2 into an overhead for students to look at as they complete their individual copies of Figure 2.2. Or show the answer key for Figure 2.2 (Figure A.4 in Appendix A) on the overhead to assist the students in completing their own maps.

Because of my hand-drawing errors, Figure 2.2 has lines that are flat and out of proportion. For example, on Figure 2.2, the distance between 20N and 30N is less than the distance between 30N and 40N. When I taught this lesson on November 20, 2008, my cooperating teacher Mr. McClanahan found maps via a Google image search for the terms "Expansion of Islam." He projected one of those maps, which was similar to the answer key for Figure 2.2 (Figure A.4) but had better-drawn lines, from his computer to a screen at the front of the room.

Students should have three colors of pens (for example black, blue, and red) and colored pencils or crayons of those same colors.

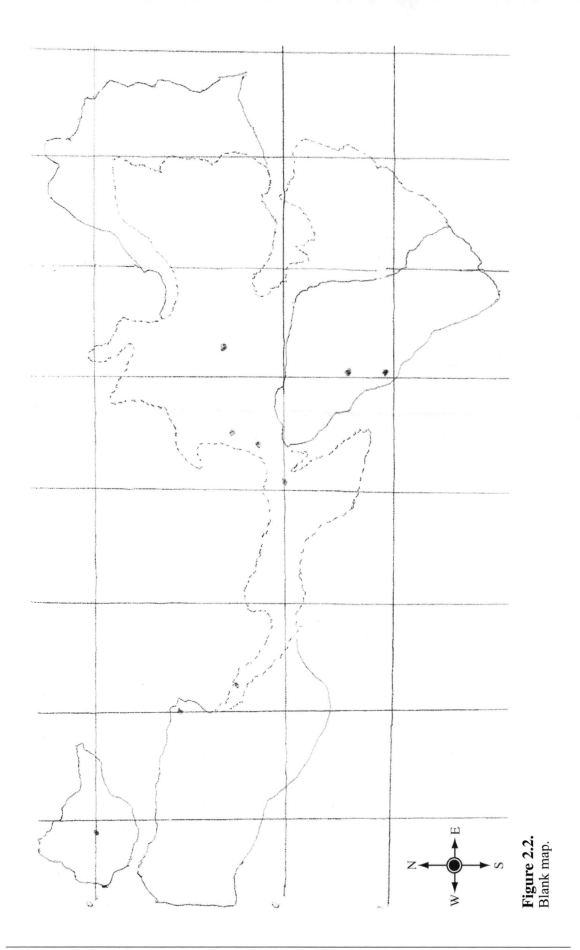

Figure 2.2.
Blank map.

From *People, Places, Checkmates: Teaching Social Studies with Chess* by Alexey W. Root. Santa Barbara, CA: Libraries Unlimited. Copyright © 2010.

Table of Latitude and Longitude

Data from Gover, 2006, pp. 163–176 (Index).

City name	Latitude (parallel)	Longitude (meridian)	Present-day country
Mecca	21N	40E	Saudi Arabia
Medina (Al Madīnah)	24N	40E	Saudi Arabia
Damascus	34N	36E	Syria
Jerusalem	32N	35E	Israel
Cairo	30N	31E	Egypt
Tripoli	33N	13E	Libya
Baghdad	33N	44E	Iraq
Toledo	40N	4W	Spain
Tunis	37N	10E	Tunisia

Figure 2.3.
Table of latitude and longitude.

From *People, Places, Checkmates: Teaching Social Studies with Chess* by Alexey W. Root. Santa Barbara, CA: Libraries Unlimited. Copyright © 2010.

Procedure

Compare maps and algebraic notation for students. State that maps and algebraic chess notation have common aspects. On a map, the longitude (vertical) lines are meridians. On a chessboard, the vertical columns are called files. The meridian line tells how far east or west a point (such as a city) is. The file (a–h) tells how far toward the **queenside** or **kingside** a square is.

On a map, the latitude (horizontal) lines are called parallels. On a chessboard, the horizontal rows are called ranks. The parallel line tells how far north or south a point (such as a city) is. The rank (1–8) tells how far toward the white side or black side of the board a square is. There are differences between geographic locators and algebraic notation. The intersection of a parallel and a meridian describes a point, whereas the intersection of a file and a rank is a square. In geography, the latitude (horizontal) measurement is given first. In chess, notation is written file-first. On some maps and all globes, latitude and longitude lines are curved. On a chessboard, files and ranks are straight. Figure 2.4 compares map and board coordinate notation systems.

Display a copy of Figure 2.2. Or display the answer key for Figure 2.2 (Figure A.4) or an image found from a Google search for "Expansion of Islam." On their own copies of Figure 2.2, students first label the parallels. The southernmost parallel shown is 20°. It runs just below the southernmost dot (Mecca). The parallel shown to the north of 20° is 30°, and the northernmost parallel shown is 40°. All are north latitude lines. Next have the students write in the longitude lines, which run from 0° (the Prime Meridian, just east of the dot marking the westernmost city, Toledo) to 70° E (the meridian furthest to the right on this map). In other words, the border lines of the map are not parallels or meridians.

Advise students to place the map's key in the southwest corner on their copies of Figure 2.2. The first color of the key designates the area of Islamic rule under Muhammad, 622–632. The second color signifies Islamic expansion from 632 to 661. The third color shows 661–732.

Using the first key color, students write in the cities of Mecca and Medina and shade the corresponding outlined area; using the second color, students write in Damascus, Jerusalem, Cairo, Tripoli, and Baghdad and shade

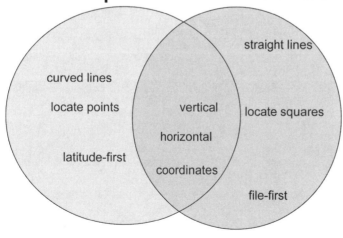

Maps versus Boards

curved lines

locate points

latitude-first

vertical

horizontal

coordinates

straight lines

locate squares

file-first

Figure 2.4.
Venn diagram comparing maps and boards.

the area; using the third color, students write in Toledo, Tunis, and Northern India and shade the remaining, outlined areas. Have the students use different colored pens for writing in the city names, and corresponding colored pencils or crayons to lightly shade the areas.

Share this historical information, and map instructions, while students complete Figure 2.2. Make sure students also have copies of Figure 2.3, or display it on an overhead projector. First, state that Muhammad preached Islam in Mecca and Medina, where he died in 632. On Figure 2.2, students locate the dots that correspond to the longitude and latitude coordinates for Mecca and Medina. Students pick one color of pen to write in the names of Mecca and Medina. Then students use a similarly colored crayon or colored pencil to shade these two cities and the area within the solid-line outlined southwestern portion of the Arabian Peninsula. Then students fill in the key with that color, indicating that area was under Muslim rule from 622 to 632.

Next, state that between 634 and 650, Muslim armies defeated the Byzantine and Persian armies, conquering Syria, Iraq, Egypt, and Iran. Students use a second color to write the names of Damascus, Jerusalem, Cairo, Tripoli, and Baghdad, and to shade the area within the dotted-line outline. They update their key with that color. List this second expansion in the map key as being from 632 to 661.

Third, state that from 711 to 715, Muslim rule extended to Spain, Turkistan, and Sind (northern India). Students use a third color to mark Toledo, Tunis, and northern India, the furthest map area outlined, and the key. This third expansion should be noted in the key as being from 661 to 732.

Cities are marked with dots on the map. Students use the parallels and meridians to determine which city name should go next to which dot. The city names, and their parallels and meridians, are on Figure 2.3.

After students complete the map, ask them to turn it over. On the back of the map, have students take notes on how Muslims interacted with conquered people in:

1. religion,
2. chess, and
3. culture and inventions.

As the Muslims conquered territories, they brought their religion and customs with them. Muslims also learned from the people that they conquered. The Qur'an (holy scripture) specifies that no one be forced to accept religion against their will (Cohen & Douglass, 2006, pp. 6, 18). Therefore, Muslims practiced tolerance of other religions. Cohen and Douglass (p. 18) wrote, "With some exceptions, Muslim leaders have adhered to this precedent over time." Those living in Muslim-controlled territories either gradually converted to Islam or remained Christians and Jews. "Muhammad often discussed religious ideas with the Jews, Christians, and polytheists (believers in many gods)" (Cohen & Douglass, p. 18).

Although the early progress of chess is associated with India, Persia, China, and Islam, "from only one of these cultures, Islam, is there a surviving chess literature which tells us in detail about the rules of the game and how it was played" (Eales, 1985, p. 19). The language of Islam is Arabic. Eales (p. 24) wrote:

> Much Persian history and literature was translated into Arabic and circulated more widely in that form. This was the background against which chess spread through the Arab world between *c.* 650 and *c.* 750–800. . . . The fact that Arabic authors as early as al-Adli seem to have been unaware of the Persian derivation of the name *shatranj* and their chess terms, though they knew that the game itself was Persian, might suggest a longer period of transition . . . with much being forgotten in the process, and something like a new beginning. (italics in the original)

Other areas of human endeavor that began, or were further developed, from 600–1000 in the Islamic Empire were: chemistry (distillation, glass manufacture), architecture (pointed arch), medicine (hospitals, surgery), mathematics (Arabic numerals and algebra), and aeronautics (parachute). More contributions of the Muslim world to civilization can be found at *1001 Inventions* (http://www.1001inventions.com/).

Evaluation

Collect maps. The answer key for the Muslim Expansion map is Figure A.4, in Appendix A. To check students' notes for accuracy use the three preceding paragraphs.

Exercise 2: Ninth-Century Chess Problem

al-Adli chess problem

White to move

Figure 2.5.
White checkmates in three moves.

Teacher Background

As mentioned in lesson 2, al-Adli was a chess author who wrote in Arabic. He was also a Muslim player of great repute. Shenk (2006, pp. 36–38) took the **problem** in Figure 2.5 from a ninth-century book by al-Adli. As noted in Figure 2.1, kings, rooks, and knights move in the same way now as in shatranj. Therefore, modern players can solve Figure 2.5 using familiar chess rules.

Procedure and Materials

Reproduce Figure 2.5 on the demonstration board, or write the following on the dry-erase board. White: Kg8; R's e1, g1; Ng3; Pf4. Black: Kf6; R's d7, h7; Ng6; Pf5. White to move and checkmate in three. Students need pencils and paper, and each pair needs a board and set.

Inform students of the procedure for solving the problem. Pairs set up the position on the board. Then each person in the pair writes in notation what they think the solution might be, by looking at the board but not moving the chessmen around yet. This thinking-and-writing step should be followed for every chess problem attempted by pairs or groups, as in exercises 4, 8, 12, and 14. Otherwise, the quicker student gives away the solution by showing it on the board, depriving his or her partner of the opportunity to think deeply about a position.

Once each person has written an answer, students take turns showing their solutions by moving the chessmen on the board. Then the pair debates which ideas look promising. After reviewing this procedure for how pairs and groups should work together, pass out sets and boards to pairs of students to work on Figure 2.5.

Expected Time

20 minutes. 5 minutes for getting out and putting away chess supplies. 10 minutes to attempt to solve the problem. 5 minutes for evaluation.

Evaluation

If students get stuck, share the first move of the solution in Appendix A. Then, with that hint, have students guess the last two moves of the solution. If any pair has solved the problem, allow them to show their solution during the next class period. Compliment pairs that allowed each person to present their ideas.

Lesson 3: Silk Road

Objectives

Students learn that each trader on the Silk Road, comprised of dozens of different trade routes, traveled less than a few hundred miles. Students dramatize the exchange of goods and money and the cultural diffusion of shatranj over the Silk Road.

NCSS Theme

VII. Production, Distribution, & Consumption.

Materials and Sources

Information and maps for lesson 3 are from Eales (1985, pp. 32–33), Geoquest (2000, map 8), Matthews (1991, pp. 16–17), Shenk (2006, p. 18), Thubron (2007, p. 24), and Neelis (2002). The definition of cultural diffusion is from a Web site ("Along the Silk Road," 1993).

Send home a copy of Figure 2.6 a week ahead of the planned date of this lesson. Ask each student to bring one item from the list, substituting fake gold and silver so as not to risk financial loss. If you do not ask students and parents for the items in Figure 2.6, you should acquire one such item for every student. Be sure to also have money (drachmas and Chinese coins); substitute more money for missing items.

Make two photocopies of Figure 2.7. One copy is for you. The other copy should be cut along the dotted lines for distribution to students for the Silk Road play.

To correctly mark Baghdad (Iraq), Merv (Mary, Turkmenistan), Samarkand (Uzbekistan), Kashgar (China), Dunhuang (China), and Chang'an (China) on your chalk- or dry-erase board, look up those cities in Silk Road Seattle (Neelis, 2002). The cities are in a line sloping gently northeast (from Baghdad to Dunhuang) and then the line turns southeast (from Dunhuang to Chang'an). Three of the cities, Merv (Mary, Turkmenistan), Samarkand (Uzbekistan), and Kashgar (China), are closer to each other than to the other cities. A rough estimation of the cities on the board would be fine, as the NCSS theme for this lesson is economics rather than geography.

Students need pencils or pens and paper.

Procedure

Collect the luxury items and money from Figure 2.6 at the front of the room. Ask why trade happens, now and in the past. Answer: Because one country or group of people wants or needs something that either cannot be produced in their own country or can be produced with less effort elsewhere. Ask students why inexpensive items were not traded. Answer: Traders had limited numbers of camels or horses to help transport goods. Therefore, the goods had to be expensive relative to their weight to make the trip profitable.

On the board, draw a line from left (west) to right (east/China). On the line, mark the cities of Baghdad (now in Iraq), Merv (now called Mary, Turkmenistan), Samarkand (now in Uzbekistan), Kashgar (China), Dunhuang (China), and Chang'an (China). Explain that the Silk Road land trade routes were active from the 5th century B.C.E. until the 10th century C.E., when water routes became more important. Also excerpt from the next four paragraphs for your students.

Within the western cities, traders bartered or exchanged goods for silver drachmas. Each trader traveled 200 miles or less before trading the goods to the next trader for transport further along the Silk Road. Every transaction increased the price of the good, as each trader needed to make a profit. Although the board shows only six major cities, there were many other cities and towns that served as oases and trading bazaars along the Silk Road. Point out the three western cities of Baghdad, Merv, and Samarkand, and the three Chinese cities of Kashgar, Dunhuang, and Chang'an.

Kashgar was a trading midpoint between the west and China. Once traders from the west arrived in Kashgar, they bartered their goods for

Luxury Items Exchanged on Silk Road Trading Routes

Goods from the west (Persia and Central Asia)	Goods from China
Glass	Silk
Gold	Bronze
Silver	Lacquer work
Gems	Ceramics
Woolen and linen fabrics	Iron
Chairs	Apricots
Vines	Oranges
Fig trees	Mulberries
Flax	Pomegranates
Jasmine	Peaches
Dates	Roses
Indian spices	Camellias
Olives	Peonies
Silver drachmas (engraved circular coins); multiple coins needed. Could substitute quarters.	Chinese coins (round coin with square hole in the middle); multiple coins needed. Could substitute hardware nuts.

Figure 2.6.
Luxury trading items.

From *People, Places, Checkmates: Teaching Social Studies with Chess* by Alexey W. Root. Santa Barbara, CA: Libraries Unlimited. Copyright © 2010.

Student 1 (scene one). Baghdad chess player, who whispers this speech, in **boldface**, about the chessmen and rules of Arabic chess to a trader (Student 2): **There is a game called shatranj. The king moves one square in any direction. The counselor moves only one diagonal square at a time. The elephant jumps to the second diagonal square. The horse moves in a capital L shape. The chariot moves on ranks and files. The foot soldier becomes a counselor when it reaches the back rank.**

Student 2 (scene one). A trader, in Baghdad, who has glass and fabrics. Student 1 whispers the rules of chess to Student 2, and later Student 2 will whisper those rules to Student 11 in Merv. Student 2 approaches Student 3, located in Baghdad. If there are horses (Students 6–10), Students 2–5, once united, will load up horses with goods. Once in Merv, Students 2–5 will bargain with Student 11, exchanging all their goods for some of the drachmas.

Student 3 (scene one). Trader with gems and gold. Student 3 joins with Student 2, and they agree to form a caravan with Students 4 and 5, approaching them from nearby in Baghdad. If there are horses (Students 6–10), Students 2–5, once united, will load up horses with goods. Once in Merv, Students 2–5 will bargain with Student 11, exchanging all their goods for some of the drachmas.

Student 4 (scene one). This trader (Student 4) carries a chair and approaches Students 2 and 3. If there are horses (Students 6–10), Students 2–5 load up horses with goods. Once in Merv, Students 2–5 will bargain with Student 11, exchanging all their goods for some of the drachmas.

Student 5 (scene one). This trader (Student 5) has spices and foods as listed in the first column of Figure 2.6. If there are horses (Students 6–10), Students 2–5 will load up horses with goods. Once in Merv, Students 2–5 will bargain with Student 11, exchanging all their goods for some of the drachmas.

Student 6 (scene one) is a horse belonging to the caravan of Students 2–5.

Student 7 (scene one) is a horse belonging to the caravan of Students 2–5.

Student 8 (scene one) is a horse belonging to the caravan of Students 2–5.

Student 9 (scene one) is a horse belonging to the caravan of Students 2–5.

Figure 2.7.
Silk Road roles for students.

Student 10 (scene one) is a horse belonging to the caravan of Students 2–5.

Student 11 (scenes one, two, and three). In Merv, the traders (Students 2–5) and horses (Students 6–10) meet another trader (Student 11) who has lots of silver drachmas. Students 2–5 bargain with Student 11 (trader), exchanging all their goods for some of the drachmas. Having heard the rules of chess from Student 2, Student 11 whispers the rules of chess to Student 12. They form a caravan to Samarkand for the end of scene two, then sit out for the beginning of scene three. At the end of scene three, in Kashgar, Students 11 and 12 will barter their goods.

Student 12 (scenes two and three). Student 12 (trader) approaches Student 11 (trader). Student 12 has goods listed in the west (left) column of Figure 2.6. Student 11 whispers the rules of chess to Student 12. They form a caravan to Samarkand for the end of scene two, then sit out for the beginning of scene three. At the end of scene three, in Kashgar, Students 11 and 12 will barter their goods.

Student 13 (scenes two and three) is a horse for Students 11 and 12. Student 13 should be loaded up with goods from 11 and 12.

Student 14 (scenes two and three) is a horse for Students 11 and 12. Student should be loaded up with goods from 11 and 12.

Student 15 (scene three) is a trader from Chang'an with a variety of goods from the right column of Figure 2.6. Student 15 will join Student 16 in a caravan and head west to Dunhuang. In Dunhuang, Students 15 and 16 sell their goods to Students 19, 20, and 21 for Chinese coins.

Student 16 (scene three) is a trader from Chang'an with a variety of goods from the right column of Figure 2.6. Student 16 will join Student 15 in a caravan and head west to Dunhuang. In Dunhuang, Students 15 and 16 sell their goods to Students 19, 20, and 21 for Chinese coins.

Student 17 (scene three) is a camel from Chang'an, loaded by Student 15 with a variety of goods from the right column of Figure 2.6. Once loaded, camel heads to Dunhuang.

Student 18 (scene three) is a camel from Chang'an, loaded by Student 16 with a variety of goods from the right column of Figure 2.6. Once loaded, camel heads to Dunhuang.

Figure 2.7.
(continued).

From *People, Places, Checkmates: Teaching Social Studies with Chess* by Alexey W. Root. Santa Barbara, CA: Libraries Unlimited. Copyright © 2010.

Student 19 (scene three) is in Dunhuang and has Chinese coins. Student 19, along with Students 20 and 21, buys goods from Chang'an caravan. Student 19 travels with Students 20 and 21 from Dunhuang to Kashgar. At the end of scene three, in Kashgar, the students barter their goods. At that point, in Kashgar, Student 19 listens to the rules of chess from Student 12.

Student 20 (scene three) is in Dunhuang and has Chinese coins. Student 20, along with Students 19 and 21, buys goods from Chang'an caravan. Student 20 travels with Students 19 and 21 from Dunhuang to Kashgar. At the end of scene three, in Kashgar, the students barter their goods.

Student 21 (scene three) is in Dunhuang and has Chinese coins. Student 21, along with Students 19 and 20, buys goods from Chang'an caravan. Student 21 travels with Students 19 and 20 from Dunhuang to Kashgar. At the end of scene three, in Kashgar, the students barter their goods.

Figure 2.7.
(continued).

Chinese goods. The traders of Chinese merchandise had acquired those goods by barter or money, sometimes leaving Chang'an for Kashgar in huge caravans of 500 or a thousand camels. Ask students why caravans were big. One answer is to protect the traders from bandits. After completing trades in Kashgar, western traders headed west with their newly acquired Chinese goods. Eastern traders returned to China with western goods.

Along with goods, the Silk Road allowed ideas and games to reach new destinations. Unlike a finished good, such as a silk jacket or a bronze statue, ideas and games were altered as they passed from person to person. Architectural evidence of this cultural diffusion is still evident today. For example, in the chief mosque of Xi'an (Chang'an), China, "the fusion of China with Islam is like artful theatre. You wander through courtyards interlocked like those of a Ming palace, where the stelae are carved alternately in Arabic or Mandarin, and a minaret rises out of a porcelain-tiled pagoda" (Thubron, 2007, p. 31). The Silk Road is an example of cultural diffusion. "In cultural diffusion, the object, item, belief, or custom changes in form or meaning in the new environment. Oftentimes, the end-product combines features of both its original and new culture" ("Along the Silk Road," 1993).

This Silk Road dramatization illustrates how shatranj might have been transmitted and transformed, as in a game of telephone, from Arab countries to China in the ninth century. An alternate historical explanation claims that chess began in China and traveled to India. Yet Chinese chess, which has different rules than western chess, "can only be proved to be in existence by *c.* 800, almost two centuries after its appearance is documented in India and Persia" (Eales, 1985, p. 33, italics in original). And Arab chess (shatranj) derives from Persian chess (chatrang), as shown in Figure 2.1.

After the lecture, assign each student to one of the roles on Figure 2.7 by passing out the card and the supplies associated with his or her role. If there are more students than trader, horse, or camel roles, the remaining students can be bandits, who try to rob the traders, or rulers, who exact tribute from trading caravans passing through their territories.

There are three scenes to this role-play. Other than students assigned to whisper the rules of chess, the acting should be in pantomime. The actors should demonstrate the narrator's words.

For scene one, students 1–11 are the actors. Everyone other than students 1–11 should sit and watch this scene. Students 1–10 (or 1–5 if you have fewer than 20 students) start in Baghdad; student 11 waits in Merv. After whispering the rules of chess to student 2, student 1 stays in Baghdad while students 2–5 walk from Baghdad toward Merv. Either the traders or their horses (students 6–10) are freshly laden with the goods. The horses may walk on all fours. If less than 20 students do not assign numbers 6–10. Students act out their parts in pantomime (trading, walking together) as you use your copy of the cards to narrate.

Figure 2.8.
Whispering rules of chess.

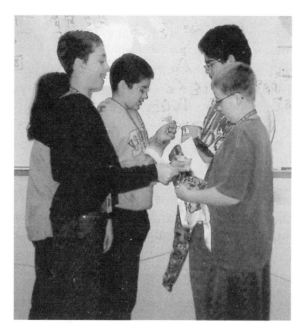

Figure 2.9.
Trading in Dunhuang.

Along with miming trades, certain students whisper about chess. After trader 2 whispers the rules of chess to trader 11, traders (2–5) and horses (6–10) head back to Baghdad. Figure 2.8 shows student 2 whispering the rules of chess to trader 11. Then students 1–10 sit down to watch scenes two and three.

For scene two, students 11–14 are needed. If you do not have enough students, eliminate the horse roles (13 and 14). After the students complete the tasks on their cards, as you narrate, the caravan (students 11–14) travels from Merv to Samarkand. Have students 11–14 take seats in the audience, but tell the class that those students will reappear in Samarkand in the middle of scene three.

For scene three, narrate that at the same time the western caravan from Merv was heading east toward Samarkand, in Chang'an two traders (students 15 and 16) with a variety of goods from the right column of Figure 2.6 and two camels (students 17 and 18, if enough students for these roles) are heading west to Dunhuang. In Dunhuang, students 15 and 16 sell their goods to students 19, 20, and 21 for Chinese coins. Figure 2.9 shows middle school students acting out trading. Students 19–21 and their camels head for Kashgar.

Traders 11–12 and their horses 13 and 14 stop watching the play and become actors again. They travel from Samarkand to Kashgar. At Kashgar the humans barter their goods. Money does not change hands, as the currency of the west and east does not match. At the same time, trader 12 whispers the rules of chess to student 19.

At this point, the students 11–21 take their new goods back in the directions from which they arrived. Have student 19 say aloud the rules of chess. Have student 1 read the Baghdad shatranj player's speech out loud to compare to the rules by the time they reached student 19. Discuss the result of this "game of telephone" in the context of the cultural diffusion definition. Note that Chinese chess today is different than western chess.

Evaluation

Ask each student to write a first-person account of his or her role on the Silk Road. Appendix A has one seventh grader's paragraph.

Exercise 3: Tandem Chess

Teacher Background

On the Internet, there are various definitions of **tandem chess.** I agree with the one offered by Jennifer Shahade (2007), "Not **bughouse!** Tandem chess is **blitz** chess with two players on each team, alternating moves. You're not allowed to talk with your partner." (Boldface added to indicate glossary entries.)

Procedure and Materials

Tandem chess requires one set and board for every four students. If chess clocks are available, set them for blitz chess. Combine one stronger chess player and one weaker chess player, or two middle-strength players, into teams. In this way, the average ability of each tandem team is about the same.

For tandem chess, one team (players 1 and 2) plays white and another team (players 3 and 4) plays black. Figure 2.10 shows a tandem team. The order of moving is 1 then 3 then 2 then 4. Then the pattern (1–3–2–4) repeats throughout the game. Players may not talk with each other. Thus, as in the Silk Road exercise, chess communication is problematic. Player 1 may make an aggressive move on the kingside, setting up a mating **attack.** If player 2 does not discern the move's intention, then he or she may retreat on the kingside.

Figure 2.10.
Tandem chess.

Expected Time

25 minutes. It takes 7 minutes to explain the rules of tandem chess, mention its connection with the Silk Road exercise, and pair the students. One game of tandem chess takes about 10 minutes. Allow another 5 minutes for getting out and putting away chess supplies, and 3 minutes for the pairs to talk with each other about how the game went.

Evaluation

After the exercise, allow pairs to discuss whether not being able to talk impaired the execution of plans. You may want to keep the list of tandem teams to have a second round, with new opponents, later.

Lesson 4: Legends around the World

Objectives

Students read aloud and analyze three legends about chess. Students record the purposes of chess in each legend. Students learn that chess has been a metaphor for war, math, love, and other aspects of culture.

NCSS Theme

IX. Global Connections.

Materials and Sources

Copies of Figure 2.11 for each group of three students. Each student needs a pencil or pen.

The sources consulted for Figure 2.11 are: for *Death of a Son,* Eales (1985, pp. 22, 25), Shenk (2006, pp. 13–14), and Yalom (2004, p. 5); for *Doubling of the Squares,* Shenk (2006, pp. 16–17) and Yalom (2004, p. 5); and for *Prince and Princess,* Yalom (2004, p. 11).

Procedure

Tell students that legends allow cultures to convey values and truths. Ask students to share a legend, past or present. Students might mention the headless horsemen, the ghost of a beheaded soldier. The headless horseman rode past a man who was on his way home from a tavern. The man was terrified, more so because he was walking past a graveyard. Ask students what values or truths the legend conveyed. Answers might include the ravages of war, hallucinations after drinking, and dangers near graveyards at night.

Legends are from many countries. *Death of a Son,* although about an Indian queen, was in the Persian (present-day Iran) epic *Book of Kings. Doubling of the Squares* is from India. The *Prince and Princess* is from *The Arabian Nights,* a collection of tales from many cultures written down in Syria.

In groups of three, each student reads aloud a different chess legend from Figure 2.11. Then the reader asks the group, "What purposes does chess serve in this legend?" The reader writes a response on the group's copy of Figure 2.11 that summarizes the group's discussion. Encourage readers to write more than one purpose of chess for each of the three legends in Figure 2.11. If there is not enough room on the front of Figure 2.11, the reader may continue writing on the back. Then it is the next reader's turn. The previous reader passes Figure 2.11 to the next reader.

Evaluation

When the groups have finished, collect Figure 2.11 for evaluation. See Appendix A for one group's answers to Figure 2.11.

Death of a Son

    In ancient India, a queen's son died from battle fatigue. The queen's council wanted to show the queen what had happened. The council asked a wise man for help. With the assistance of a carpenter, the wise man created chess. The wise man and the carpenter played a chess game for the queen. At the end of the game, one king was in *shāh māt,* a Persian term that means the king is exhausted. Thus, the queen learned that her son died of battle fatigue rather than at the hands of another soldier. The purposes of chess in *Death of a Son*: _____

_____

Doubling of the Squares

    A wise man invented chess and presented it to an Indian king. The king was delighted with the game and asked its inventor to name a reward. The wise man asked for 1 grain of wheat on the 1st square of the chessboard, 2 on the 2nd, 4 on the 3rd, and that the doubling of grains continue in this pattern until the 64th square. When the king realized that 18 quintillion grains would be needed, he learned an important lesson. The purposes of chess in *Doubling of the Squares*: _____

_____

Prince and Princess

    A Muslim prince plays chess against a Christian princess. During the game, he is distracted by her beautiful face and loses. They fall in love, and the Christian princess is converted to Islam. The purposes of chess in *Prince and Princess*: _____

_____

Figure 2.11.
Three chess legends.

Exercise 4: Mongolian Chess Legend

Figure 2.12.
Bayaraa Zorigt.

Teacher Background

Exercise 4 is from University of Texas at Dallas (UTD) student Bayaraa Zorigt, whose photo is in Figure 2.12. She retold this legend while enrolled in my Chess in Education Certificate Online courses. Bayaraa is a UTD chess team member. The **Fédération Internationale des Échecs (FIDE)** awarded her the title of **Woman FIDE master (WFM)**. Bayaraa also has a **rating** of **master** from the **United States Chess Federation (USCF)**. When Bayaraa was a child, her grandfather bought her a storybook called the *Mongolian Traditional Myth.* Most of the stories in the book are 100 to 600 years old. She clearly remembered the story "Uranber's Checkmate." It is about a clever wife, Uranber, who helped her husband by telling a secret prompt. She shared the hint when her husband was having a hard time playing chess with their landlord.

Procedure and Materials

Read this story, a retelling of "Uranber's Checkmate," aloud to your students. Once upon a time there was a herder, who had a very clever and beautiful wife named Uranber. One day the landlord came to their house and forced her husband to play chess with a high bet. If the landlord lost the game, he promised to give a huge amount of land and a lot of gold to the herder. But the landlord said that if the herder lost the game, he should give his wife. They played a long game without food and sleep. When the game was about to finish, Uranber's husband was in a critical situation.

Uranber saw the position and told her husband, "Our two children already grew up. Let's break our chariots, mount the children on a camel, and save us from the famine." Her secret prompt's meaning was to **sacrifice** the two rooks, and move the bishop on a square to checkmate the king when a pawn's move uncovers the bishop's power. Her husband thought and thought, and then he found the solution and won.

This story, from the ancient time of Mongolia, is still told today. It teaches that women should not only be beautiful, but also have to be smart and critical. Also, it teaches that girls and women can play chess very well.

Ask your students to find the chess moves that Uranber conveyed to her husband. The problem in Figure 2.13 uses modern (post-1475) chess

Uranber chess problem

White to move

Figure 2.13.
"Uranber's Checkmate"
chess problem.

rules. The checkmate sequence is four moves long. Reproduce Figure 2.13 on the demonstration board. If you do not have a demonstration board, write the following on the dry-erase board: White (the herder): Ka1; R's h1, h3; Bh2; P's f6, g6. Black (the landlord): Kg8; Qc2; P's c3, d3. White to move and checkmate in four.

Pass out sets and boards so that students can try to solve the problem, either as pairs or individually. If students are working as pairs, each pair sets up the position on the board. Students need pencils or pens, and notebook paper or score sheets. Then each student should write his or her solution individually before sharing ideas and moving the chessmen around. Observe that each student in the pair presents his or her ideas.

Expected Time

20 minutes. 5 minutes to read "Uranber's Checkmate." 5 minutes for chess supplies. 10 minutes for solving, or attempting to solve, the problem.

Evaluation

If students get stuck, share the first two moves of the solution in Appendix A. With that hint, have students try again to find the last two moves of the solution. You may show the entire solution at the end of class or delay showing it until a later time. Compliment pairs that allowed each person to present their ideas.

Lesson 5: Write a Legend

Objectives

Students learn that a legend is a realistic story that solves a problem and teaches facts or values. Students write a legend.

NCSS Theme

IV. Individual Development & Identity.

Materials and Sources

Pencil or pen and paper for each student. Optional: set and board for each student; copies of Kennedy (2008) as examples of chess problems turned into stories.

If the lesson is going to be taught in one class period, display a copy of Figure 2.11 using an overhead projector. If more class periods are available, have students spend one class period reading legends at the school library. Later, students may adapt those legends for chess (perhaps the Headless Horseman becomes the Headless Chessman).

Procedure

Ask students which human activities have inspired writers throughout history. Some answers might be war, love, trade, exploration, social hierarchy, and raising children. Ask which of these phenomena might be represented by chess. Recalling Figure 2.11, which can be displayed on an overhead projector, students might answer that chess can demonstrate war, as in *Death of a Son*. Chess might show love, as between the players in *Prince and Princess*. Arabic legends of the 9th and 10th century said that chess was invented "to educate a prince, to replace war, or to occupy the time of a king who, like Alexander, had defeated all his enemies within reach and was at a loss for something destructive to do" (Eales, 1985, p. 26).

In the legends in Figure 2.11, chess solved a problem. Chess explained a son's death to his mother, the queen. In *Prince and Princess,* chess brought together two people of different religions. The *Doubling of the Squares* memorably explained geometric progression.

Ask each student to select a human activity, and a problem that arises in that activity. For example, one area of human activity is war. A problem is that people get killed. A legend might be created that chess was invented as a nonlethal substitute for war. Tell students that, unlike a myth, supernatural events or gods are not usually involved in legends. A legend should be a believable, though not necessarily true, narrative. Chess legends written using this methodology do not require the writer to know the rules of chess. If the lesson is to be taught in one class session, end the lecture here by asking students to write a legend similar to those in Figure 2.11.

If more class sessions are available, take students to the library to read or check out books of legends. During our advisory visit to the SMS library, each student read two legends and took notes on a form. Figure A.8 (within Appendix A) shows that form, and a seventh grader's notes written on it.

When you return from the library, discuss what legends were read and how they could be adapted to chess. If your students are intermediate chess players, additional class time might be for looking at chess problems such as the two problems included in this lesson or those in Kennedy (2008). While some writers likely began their legends by thinking about love, war, or death, chess-playing writers might begin with a chess problem and then write a legend to explain the problem's solution. "Uranber's Checkmate," from exercise 4, may have begun as a four-move chess problem. The writer probably added the story of the landlord, tenant, and wife to give hints about the problem's solution.

For legend-writing inspiration, for intermediate students, here are two chess problems created by **International Master (IM)** Doug Root. Because there are very few chessmen in these two problems, writers might personify each piece and pawn.

1. White: Kh5, Pf7; Black: Kh7. White to move and checkmate in six. Solution: **1. f8(R)** Under-**promoting** to a rook is the key to solving the problem, since promoting to a queen would have been stalemate.

Black has some choices of next moves, but checkmate will follow because a king and rook can win against a lone king. **1....Kg7 2. Rf5 Kh7 3. Rf7+ Kh8 4. Kg6 Kg8 5. Rf5 Kh8 6. Rf8# 1–0.**

2. White: Kg6, Na7, Nb8. Black: Kg8, Pa6. White to move and checkmate in five. **1. Nd7.** This move restricts the black king to just two squares, g8 and h8. Then white maneuvers his knights for checkmate before black can promote his pawn. **1....a5 2. Nc6 a4 3. Ne7+ Kh8 4. Ne5 a3 5. Nf7# 1–0.**

Each student's legend can be as short as three sentences, and have no chess notation, as in Figure 2.11's *Prince and Princess.* Or a chess version of a familiar legend could be written, such as the Headless Chessman. Or the legend could be based on a chess problem, such as one of the two Doug Root problems, and include chess notation.

Evaluation

Most of the legends written in one class period will be short, as are the legends in Figure 2.11. An example of such a short legend, written by a rising fifth grader, is in Appendix A. If more class periods are spent on lesson 5, the legends may be more elaborate and may contain chess problems. Evaluate whether the final draft is a legend, and whether chess serves one or more purposes. And, if the legend is connected to a chess problem, does the writing explain the chess moves? Three of my students' legends, two of them written after library and classroom preparation sessions and completion of exercises 5-A and 5-B, are in Appendix A.

Exercise 5-A: Create a Problem

Teacher Background

Refer to Figures 2.1 and 2.11 for background about how pieces moved before 1475 and some ideas for chess myths. Make copies of Figure 2.14, enough for each problem-creator student (or pair of students) to have one copy of Figure 2.14.

Procedure and Materials

Have copies of Figures 2.1, 2.11, and 2.14 available. Ask each student to create a chess problem to accompany one of the legends in Figure 2.11. Remind students that if the legend is set before 1475, only the king, knight, and rook have the same moves as today, except **castling** did not exist. The pawn could move only one square at a time. Rules for other pieces are in Figure 2.1.

Give each student a board and set. If you do not have enough chess supplies, or wish students to partner up for other reasons, give a board and set to pairs or groups instead of individuals. Students document their problems on copies of Figure 2.14. Pencils or pens are required.

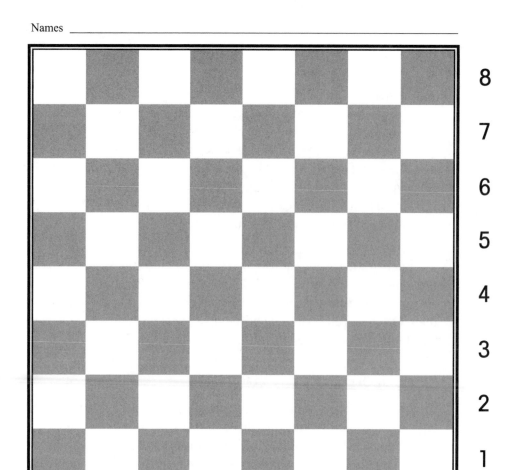

To make a diagram of a position, use the following abbreviations: P for white pawn,

N for white knight, B for white bishop, R for white rook, Q for white queen, and K for white king.

For example, a white rook on e4 is recorded by a letter R written on the e4 square.

Use the same abbreviations for black pieces and pawns, but circle them to show that a

black piece or pawn is represented. For example, black rook on e6 is recorded by a ® (a circled

letter R) on e6. Be sure to state which side is to move (white or black) at the bottom of this page.

Figure 2.14.
Blank chess diagram.

Expected Time

25 minutes. 5 minutes for chess supplies. 20 minutes for creating and recording their problems.

Evaluation

In Appendix A is a chess problem that matches the *Death of a Son* legend from Figure 2.11.

Exercise 5-B: Robin Hood and the Pawn

Teacher Background

My daughter Clarissa, shown in Figure 2.15 with my rabbit Abba, gave me the idea of adapting the Robin Hood legend to represent the king and pawn against king chess exercise.

Exercise 5-B combines a quasi-historical figure (Robin Hood) with a plausible story about him (a legend) that teaches a chess concept (king and pawn against king win). When I taught exercise 5-B in January of 2009, my students were in the process of creating their lesson 5 chess legends.

Exercise 5-B taught my new students, and reviewed for my returning students, how to promote a pawn when opposed by a king. See also Root (2009b, Appendix D), which gives a different analogy and continues after the promotion to show the checkmate.

There are many sources on the legend of Robin Hood. The stiff penalty for killing a deer in Sherwood Forest is from Curry (1994).

Procedure and Materials

Reproduce Figure 2.16 on the demonstration board. Or write on the dry-erase board, White: Ke3; Pe2. Black: Kd5. White to move.

Figure 2.15.
Clarissa Root, age 15, and Abba, age 6.

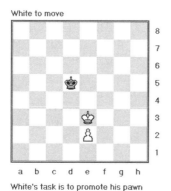

White to move

White's task is to promote his pawn

Figure 2.16.
Robin Hood (white) vs.
Sheriff of Nottingham
(black).

Tell the legend of Robin Hood or ask your students what they know of Robin Hood from movies or books. Legend portrays Robin Hood as a noble outlaw who robs the rich and gives to the poor. Robin Hood stories are set in 13th-century England, in Sherwood Forest. The Sheriff of Nottingham collects high taxes and administers stiff penalties. For example, the deer in Sherwood Forest belong to King John. So taking a deer is punishable by prison time, if the perpetrator is caught by the Sheriff.

In the legend of Robin Hood and the Pawn, the pawn represents a stag (male deer) that Robin wants to bring to a poor family. The Sheriff of Nottingham is the black king, and Robin Hood is the white king. The e-file is a passage through Sherwood Forest to the poor family's home on e8. The white king, Robin Hood, must control the e-file without letting the black king see the deer. When the chess moves commence, Robin Hood dazzles the Sheriff with fancy footwork and archery. At the same time, Robin Hood hides the stag behind him. **1. Kf4 Ke6.** The black king is blocking the way to safety. In the next sequence of moves, the white king uses the **opposition** to drive the black king out of e-file. Likewise, Robin Hood outmaneuvers the Sheriff. **2. Ke4 Kd6 3. Kf5 Ke7 4. Ke5 Ke8 5. Ke6 Kf8.** Now that the black king has stepped aside, the pawn can advance. **6. e4 Ke8 7. e5 Kd8 8. Kf7.** This move controls the promotion square of e8. Here Robin Hood has his Merry Men blindfold the Sheriff, so that the stag can be hustled past him. **8....Kd7 9. e6+** In this first encounter between the pawn and black king, the white king protects the white pawn and the two squares it needs to promote. Therefore, he makes sure the white pawn cannot be captured. The black king is now powerless to prevent delivery of the pawn (stag) to e8 (the poor family's home). He blindly steps aside. **9....Kd8 10. e7+ Kd7 11. e8(Q)+,** and white can win with king and queen against black king.

Each pair of students needs a set and a board. Have each pair play out the position with each other until they feel confident about the pattern. If students have previously learned the king and queen against king checkmate, students should continue until checkmate.

Expected Time

30 minutes. 5 minutes for chess supplies. 10 minutes for your lecture at the demonstration board. 15 minutes for students to practice Figure 2.16 with their partners and be tested (see Evaluation).

Evaluation

Individually test each student on Figure 2.16 against you, using a set and board. See Figure 1.7, column 4, for my students' test results promoting the pawn, then checkmating with the resulting king and queen against king.

Chapter 3

CHESS AND SOCIETY

Modern chess rules evolved after chess arrived in Western Europe. In lesson 6, students compare the older, slow-paced game of chess to modern chess. For lesson 7, students dramatize the skills, which included chess, of noblemen and noblewomen. During lesson 8, students respond to historical accounts about the recall of Columbus, perhaps because of a chess game. In lesson 9, students debate whether the Turk Chess Automaton was a good use of technology. For lesson 10, students design sets of federal leaders.

Although the lessons in this chapter may be taught in any order, exercise 7 builds on exercise 6. Therefore, teach exercise 6 before exercise 7. Both exercise 6 and exercise 7 use the premodern rules of chess. Exercises 8, 9, and 10 use modern chess rules.

Lesson 6: Rule Changes

Objectives

Students describe changes in values, beliefs, and attitudes from having faster chess games and faster technology.

NCSS Theme

VIII. Science, Technology, & Society.

Materials and Sources

I consulted Yalom (2004) about the role of chess in medieval courtship, both before and after the chess queen acquired her new powers in 1475.

For student materials for this lesson, find a news story about some type of modern technology (cell phone, Internet, text messaging, etc.) and its effect on Americans. For example, select a press release from *Pew Internet & American Life Project* (http://www.pewinternet.org/) for students to read online or for you to print for them. If printing, make enough copies so that each student has a copy. Students need pencils or pens and notebook paper.

Procedure

Have the students read a news story or a Pew press release about the impact of technology on American values, beliefs, and attitudes. Answers in brackets are the ones most likely to be given after completing the reading. Ask students if the cited technology made communication faster. [Yes.] Ask students if technology permitted communication that was not face-to-face. [Yes.]

Tell students that in the medieval era (500–1500 C.E.) an unmarried man and an unmarried woman were rarely alone together. Usually, courtship required letters, or interactions under the watchful eye of a chaperone. In contrast, "chess provided an excuse for lovers to meet in the intimacy of gardens and boudoirs, where they could spar with their feelings as well as their chessmen" (Yalom, 2004, p. 126).

After the rules changed in 1475, chess became a fast, competitive game unsuited for courtship. Summarize for your students what Yalom (2004, pp. 228–229) wrote:

> Ironically enough, it may be that the elevation of the chess queen and the bishop to new levels of strength had something to do with the dwindling number of female participants. Once those two pieces acquired a greater range of **mobility,** it took fewer moves, on average, to complete a match. New chess was no longer suited to leisurely encounters between ladies and gentlemen that could last a day or more. . . . Hands had to be ready to grasp a piece on the board, and not a knee under the table. Chess would no longer tolerate dalliance of any sort.
>
> As chess became less social and more competitive, the professional chess player arrived on the scene. Forget the troubadour chess partner or the attentive lover or even the town Wunderkind who was allowed to take time off after the harvest to play with the local lord. Now there were full-time champions earning their living from arranged matches in princely settings throughout Europe. (Boldface added to indicate glossary entry.)

Evaluation

Ask students to reflect on the technology discussed in their assigned readings. That technology might be: high-speed Internet, cell phones, online shopping, social networking sites such as MySpace, or communication through text messaging. Assign each student to write a paragraph comparing how values, beliefs, and attitudes changed after adoption of this new technology to what happened to courtship and chess after the rule changes in 1475. A seventh grader's paragraph is in Appendix A.

Exercise 6: Slow-Paced Chess

Teacher Background

Since you will be stopping the games at the 15-minute mark, students might not promote pawns. Therefore, you may not need to highlight the promotion information in the next section. Have copies of Figure 2.1 available, or display Figure 2.1 on an overhead projector.

Procedure and Materials

Tell students that, before 1475, the bishop moved by jumping to a second **diagonal** square. It never occupied the first diagonal square. For example, a bishop on the f1 square could move only to d3 or h3, although it could leap an intervening man on e2 or g2. It was similar to a pawn in value. Also, before 1475, pawns moved just one square at a time. The firzan (or vizier, or counselor), the queen's predecessor, moved only one diagonal square at a time.

Upon promotion, each pawn could become a firzan. Therefore, one could have multiple firzans. The firzan got a new name (queen) in northern Europe around 1000, and that new name slowly spread through Europe in the following centuries. Yet the queen and the firzan had exactly the same moves before 1475.

Either write the rules from column 4 of Figure 2.1 on the dry-erase board or ask students to refer to their Figure 2.1 copies. Although the queen, bishop, and pawn got their full powers after 1475, it was not until the early- to mid-1600s that castling rules became firmly established in western Europe.

Each pair of students needs a set and a board. Have students play a game of chess using the rules from before 1475. That is, they use their modern sets but follow the rules from column 4 of Figure 2.1.

Expected Time

25 minutes. 5 minutes for supplies. 5 minutes for procedures and evaluation. 15 minutes for playing.

Evaluation

Interrupt the games after 15 minutes to discuss the following questions. Likely answers are in brackets. First, was **en passant** possible? [No.] If not, why not? [En passant is only possible when a pawn does a double-jump on a file adjacent to an enemy pawn.] Second, did the game seem slower or faster than games using modern rules? [Slower. It took longer to attack or control the **center** because pawns only moved one square at a time. Also, the firzan, unlike the modern (post-1475) queen, was not a powerful attacking piece.] Third, ask the students the advantages or disadvantages of the slower pace. [One advantage might be that, if one is losing, it would take longer for the other player to win. As indicated in lesson 6, games that take a long time also allow for extended social interaction. One disadvantage might be that the game is slower and perhaps more boring.]

Lesson 7: Noble Charades

Objectives

Students portray the appearances and expected skills of noblemen and noblewomen. Optional extension: Students discuss what clothing and skills are expected of them as members of a group (for example, as middle school students in the United States).

NCSS Theme

V. Individuals, Groups, & Institutions.

Materials and Sources

Copies of Figure 3.1, one per student. Or use an overhead projector to display Figure 3.1. The table in Figure 3.1 is paraphrased from Yalom (2004, pp. 94–95). Optional: If you have additional information about skills of the nobility (Europe, 12th–16th centuries), have students take notes from you (or from a text) to create an extended table for Figure 3.1. For this option, students need pens or pencils. You might also display illustrations of noble clothing.

Procedure

As students arrive for class, have them silently study Figure 3.1. After they have studied for two or three minutes, ask if there are questions about how nobles dressed or about any of the skills. For example, some students might ask for a definition of falconry.

Optional: If you have additional skills of the nobility to add to the table in Figure 3.1, have students extend the table on their copies of Figure 3.1 or on notebook paper.

Being a member of a group (the nobility) influenced clothing and the type of skills one was expected to have. Extension: Ask students what groups they belong to, and whether a certain look or particular skills are expected of them because of their group or institutional membership. For example, do middle school students in the United States wear jeans or know how to write a five-paragraph essay?

For charades, divide the students into two teams, which I will call team A and team B. One person will be selected from team A to be an actor. For each turn, team A and team B need a spokesperson who is not the actor. The instructor will time (with a clock or watch), and keep score

Clothing for nobility in the Middle Ages had "rich, trailing garments and elaborate headdresses for women, and short tunics with wide sleeves and long, pointed shoes for the men" (Rowland-Warne, 1992, p. 14).

STUDY THE TABLE OF THE SKILLS OF AN IDEAL NOBLE, IN THE 12TH THROUGH 16TH CENTURIES IN EUROPE.

Ideal Noblewoman	Ideal Nobleman
falconry	falconry
chess	chess
stitch on silk and brocade	horseback riding
writing verse and poetry	martial arts
backgammon	backgammon
singing	hunting
playing the lyre	dice

Figure 3.1.
Skills of noblewomen and noblemen.

From *People, Places, Checkmates: Teaching Social Studies with Chess* by Alexey W. Root. Santa Barbara, CA: Libraries Unlimited. Copyright © 2010.

on the dry-erase board or chalkboard. I recommend hiding Figure 3.1 before beginning charades, to make the game more challenging.

Introduce the procedure and scoring system for noble charades. The instructor whispers the gender of the member of the nobility and the skill to be mimed to an actor from team A. That actor then uses gestures and movement, but not voice, to portray a nobleman or a noblewoman performing that particular skill. The actor's teammates whisper guesses to the team A spokesperson, who then voices the official team guesses. Multiple guesses are allowed within the 10-second limit. If team A guesses the correct answer within 10 seconds, it gets two points. If its guess is wrong, team B's spokesperson has 2 seconds to steal by guessing correctly. The first guess by the stealing team's spokesperson counts as the official, and only, try. A correct guess earns one point for the stealing team. Then it is time for an actor from team B, and the procedure repeats.

Evaluation

The instructor observes students acting and guessing. Charades indicate if students have learned the information in Figure 3.1.

Exercise 7: Chess with Dice

Teacher Background

Read exercise 6 and Figure 2.1 for the rules of chess before 1475.

Procedure and Materials

Either write the rules from column 4 of Figure 2.1 on the dry-erase board or ask students to refer to their Figure 2.1 copies. Review the rules as stated in exercise 6.

According to historian David Shenk, the slow-paced rules were okay with the Muslims, but the Europeans wanted a faster game. As Shenk (2006, pp. 58–59) wrote:

> To speed up the game, alternative versions had emerged wherein one die would be thrown before each move to determine which piece would be played:
> If it landed on "1," the player would move a Pawn.
> If on "2," a Knight.
> If on "3," a Bishop.
> If on "4," a Rook.
> If on "5," the Queen.
> If on "6," the King

My interpretations follow. If the die (singular of dice) asks you to move a chessman that you cannot legally move, then you lose your turn. That is, the other player gets to roll and move. If your die roll does not allow you

Figure 3.2.
Chess with dice.

to escape from check, you lose if your opponent manages to roll a move that captures your king. As in chess, you cannot move your king to an attacked square or make a move that exposes him to check.

Each pair of students needs a set, a die, and a board. Have students play a game of chess using the rules from before 1475. In other words, the queen moves like a firzan (vizier or counselor) and the bishop moves like a fil (elephant). The only difference from exercise 6 is that the roll of a die determines which chessman moves. Figure 3.2 shows a student throwing the die for his next move.

Expected Time

25 minutes. 5 minutes for supplies. 5 minutes for procedures and evaluation. 15 minutes for playing.

Evaluation

Interrupt the games after 15 minutes to discuss whether the die changed the pacing, as compared to exercise 6. Ask whether students liked the introduction of chance into chess. Discuss the Shenk quote (2006, p. 59), "fate had been invited into humanity's great symbolic arena of skill and free will."

Lesson 8: Chess Legend of Columbus

Objectives

Students define primary and secondary sources. Students respond to secondary sources about the recall of Columbus.

NCSS Theme

II. Time, Continuity, & Change.

Materials and Sources

For the Washington Irving paragraph and the Augustus Goodyear Heaton painting, visit the Senate Art Web page ("Recall of Columbus," 2008). Clicking on the painting enlarges it. Make two or three large color copies of the painting, or display it on a computer screen. Make copies of the paragraph written by Irving, enough for at least half the class. Have notebook paper and writing utensils available for students who want to write, and blank paper and colored pencils available for students who wish to draw.

A map showing Granada, Spain, Portugal, and France could be referred to during your lecture. You might also show the Indies, which in Columbus's time referred to all lands to the east of the Indus River ("Christopher Columbus," 2008).

Procedure

Lecture about the events leading up to the recall of Columbus. In 1484, Columbus asked the king of Portugal to fund his proposed voyage to sail west to get to the east (the Indies). The king turned him down. So, for seven years prior to 1492, Columbus made requests of King Ferdinand of Aragón and Queen Isabella of Castile. In early 1492, rejected again by Ferdinand and Isabella's court (camped in Santa Fe because of the war to conquer Granada from the Moors), Columbus headed north to appeal to the king of France.

As Columbus crossed a small bridge near Granada, about six miles from the court in Santa Fe, a royal messenger overtook him with the news that Ferdinand and Isabella had changed their minds. Ask students, "Why do you think the king and queen recalled Columbus?" Yalom (2004) quoted a 19th-century translation of letters, the originals of which were purportedly written by an eyewitness in Ferdinand and Isabella's court. The letters stated that Ferdinand approved Columbus's voyage because Ferdinand was in a good mood from winning a chess game. Yalom (2004, p. 255) suspected that the letters are not authentic because they contained the modern phrase "new world" instead of "East Indies."

The letters, if genuine, would be a primary source because they were written at the time of the event. Ask students to define primary and secondary sources, and correct their definitions as necessary. Paraphrasing the Web site "Primary vs Secondary Sources" (http://www.princeton.edu/~refdesk/primary2.html), a primary source is a document or physical object created during the time under study. Primary sources include diaries, speeches, manuscripts, letters, interviews, news videos, autobiographies, and official records. Also included are creative works such as poetry or novels and artifacts such as clothing or furniture. In contrast, a secondary source interprets and analyzes primary sources. Secondary sources may have pictures, quotes, or graphics from primary sources in them. Secondary sources include textbooks, magazine articles, histories, criticisms, commentaries, and encyclopedias.

Tell students they will be reading and viewing two 19th-century secondary sources, a paragraph of writing and a painting, about the recall of Columbus. Ask students if they wish to make a drawing after reading one paragraph of Washington Irving's book. Or ask them if they would prefer writing a paragraph after viewing the Augustus Goodyear Heaton painting. Group the students according to their preferences. Give copies of the paragraph, located at the end of the Web page ("Recall of Columbus," 2008), to those students who wish to read then draw.

Let the other students view the painting, either on a computer screen or sharing prints, and each write their own paragraph about it.

Evaluation

Have students who drew look at the Heaton painting. Have students who wrote read the Irving paragraph. Ask them to compare their products with those of Heaton and Irving. Products by my SMS chess advisory students are in Appendix A.

Then read aloud the parts of the Web site ("Recall of Columbus," 2008) that tell how Irving and Heaton researched the recall of 1492 to create their secondary sources. Representative quotes include: "Heaton had confirmed visual details of the story by visiting the Columbus site in Granada and by making a careful study of period costume." Irving worked "in Spain from newly discovered original documents."

Exercise 8: King Ferdinand and Queen Isabella

Teacher Background

Yalom (2004, p. 209) reproduced the alleged Ferdinand versus Fonesca chess position, in which Ferdinand's win put him in a good mood and therefore led to him recalling Columbus. The translated letters, which included this chess position, were in the European chess journal *Le Palamède,* October 15, 1845. Isabella may also have been the inspiration for the new, more powerful moves of the queen. Yalom (2004, p. 211) wrote:

> Off and on for more than two decades, from 1469 to 1492, Isabella and Ferdinand were engaged in combating their enemies. It was during this period that "new chess" featuring the formidable queen came into being. A militant queen more powerful than her husband had arisen in Castile; why not on the chessboard as well?

Procedure and Materials

Demonstration board or dry-erase board to display Figure 3.3. If using a dry-erase board, write, White: Ka8; R's f5, g4; Bh3; P's b4, e6. Black: Kc8; Qe1; R's c1, h8; Nb3; Pc7. White to move and checkmate in four.

Tell students that, as with "Uranber's Checkmate" in exercise 4, a husband wins because of a hint from his wife. Quoting Yalom's translation of the European chess journal article:

Isabella drew near the King. She even leaned on his shoulder and held back his arm at the very moment when, after having hesitated for a long time, he raised his hand to place his rook in the fifth square.

"My Lord," she said, "I think you have won."

White to move

Checkmate in four moves

Figure 3.3.
Ferdinand versus Fonesca.

"I hope so," Ferdinand answered. He stopped and began to reflect again. (Yalom, 2004, pp. 208–209)

After pausing, he found the four-move checkmate.

Inform students of the procedure for solving the problem. After setting up the position on the board, each person in the pair will write in notation what they think the solution might be. Then each person will take turns showing his or her solution on the chessboard. After each person has presented, the pair can move the chessmen around and debate which ideas look promising. During class, observe pairs to make sure this procedure is followed.

Pass out sets and boards to pairs of students to work on the solution. Students need pens or pencils, and notebook paper or score sheets.

Expected Time

20 minutes. 5 minutes for supplies. 2 minutes for giving the introduction to the problem. 10 minutes for solving the problem and writing the solution in algebraic notation. 3 minutes for reviewing the solution with the class.

Evaluation

If any pair has solved the Figure 3.3 problem, allow them to show their solution during the next class period. If the pairs have not solved the problem, you may present the solution from Appendix A. Compliment pairs that allowed each person a chance to present their ideas.

Lesson 9: The Turk, Automaton Chess Player

Objective

Students debate whether technological deception is acceptable if the end result is entertainment.

Figure 3.4.
The Turk Chess Automaton.

NCSS Theme

VIII. Science, Technology, & Society.

Materials and Sources

Standage (2002) is a nonfiction account of the Turk. Löhr (2005/2007) is a novel. Both sources address deception through technology, an ethical question raised by the Turk. Conduct a Google Image search for "Turk Chess Automaton" and find an image that shows the Turk but not how it works. One such image is Figure 3.4 (Wichary, 2006). Display this image at the start of your lecture to illustrate the appearance of the Turk.

For the end of your lecture, show the Turk's inner workings through images or through YouTube or other videos.

Figure 3.5 is a template for the debate exercise. Photocopy Figure 3.5 (one copy per student). Students also need pens or pencils.

Procedure

Give students a brief history of the Turk and display your initial Turk image. Quoting Root (2008a, p. 10):

> Hungarian nobleman Wolfgang von Kempelen declared to Empress Maria Theresa that he could out-do the 1769 performance of a French conjurer. The empress gave him six months paid leave, and Kempelen returned with the Turk, purportedly an automaton chess-player. . . . During Kempelen's life, the Turk's secret was guessed at but not revealed.

The empress, and many others, believed that the human-sized torso of the Turk was an automaton. The Turk rolled its eyes. Its arm moved pieces. After Kempelen died, the Turk had other owners. The Turk defeated famous historical figures such as Benjamin Franklin and Napoleon Bonaparte. In an essay that "is widely regarded as the prototype for his later mystery stories," Edgar Allen Poe speculated about the Turk's inner workings (Standage, 2002, p. 183). Spectators paid to watch the Turk play chess.

Ask students how they think the Turk operated. Was it a robot or an early chess computer? Then tell them the Turk's secret and show images or videos of its inner workings. The cabinet at the base of the Turk's torso had multiple doors. The exhibitor always opened those doors in a particular order so that the Turk's operator, usually a chess master, would remain hidden. Using advanced technology for the 18th century, that hidden operator manipulated levers and pointers to move the Turk's left arm. The chessmen had magnets attached to hidden wires and disks. The operator determined his opponent's move by noticing which disks wobbled. The operator had the knight's tour written out so that the Turk could demonstrate it as a command performance.

In the main part of this lesson, students debate the pros and cons of the statement, "The Turk, though deceptive, was a good use of technology." To assign roles for this debate have the class number off (1, 2, 3, 4, etc.) to divide the class in half. Students assigned an odd number (1, 3, 5, 7, etc.) become debaters in favor of the Turk. Students with an even number (2, 4, 6, 8, etc.) become debaters against the Turk. Tell students to remember their assigned numbers. Distribute copies of Figure 3.5 to remind students of their roles. The pro team has 5–10 minutes to prepare each of its debaters to state one pro point. Each pro debater writes a prepared debate statement on the back of his or her copy of Figure 3.5. At the same time, the con team prepares its debaters. Each con debater writes a prepared debate statement on the back of his or

Debate topic, "The Turk, though deceptive, was a good use of technology." Before the debate begins, each debater writes a prepared statement (pro or con, depending on the number assigned to the debater) on the back of this page.

Pro (odd-numbered debaters)	Con (even-numbered debaters)
Debater #1: States why the Turk was a good use of technology, using his or her prepared statement on the back of this page. Debater #2 listens. At the end of the debate, Debater #1 will respond to the final con student's point.	Debater #2: Refute Debater #1's point. Presents his or her prepared point from the back of this page. Debater #3 should be listening to Debater #2, to get ready to respond.
Debater #3: Refutes con point from Debater #2. Makes pro statement on why the Turk was a good use of technology, using his or her prepared statement on the back of this page. Next con debater listens.	Debater #4: Refute Debater #3's point. Presents his or her prepared con point from the back of this page. Debater #5 should be listening to Debater #4, to get ready to respond.
Debater #5: Refutes con point from Debater #4. Makes pro statement on why the Turk was a good use of technology; using his or her prepared statement on the back of this page. Next con debater listens.	Debater #6: Refute Debater #5's point. Presents his or her prepared con point from the back of this page. Debater #7 should be listening to Debater #6, to get ready to respond.

Pattern in chart continues, up to the number of students in class. Final con debater is refuted by Debater #1.

Figure 3.5.
Debate template.

her copy of Figure 3.5. Debaters bring their copies of Figure 3.5 to the debate area.

Evaluation

Line up the pro and con debaters across from each other in numerical order. Have the first pro debater make his or her statement. The second debater refutes the pro point then presents his con point. Then the third debater refutes the con point then presents her pro point, and so forth. The final con debater's point is refuted by the first pro debater, to end the debate.

Exercise 9: Endgame Problem from the Turk

Teacher Background

Standage (2002, p. 152) gives the following **endgame** problem from New York, 1826. On that leg of the United States tour, challengers selected a position from the Turk's book of endgames. The Turk got the first move in whatever position was selected, which meant that it had the winning chances. Another reason for the abbreviated challenges is that the Turk's operator had a difficult job. The candle inside his chamber gradually used up the oxygen, so Turk games had to be one hour or less.

Procedure and Materials

Demonstration board or dry-erase board to display Figure 3.6. If using a dry-erase board, write, White: Kh3; P's a5, b4, c4. Black: Ka6; P's f5, g5, h4. Tell students to give white the first move, and to take turns playing white. Do not tell students whether white wins, loses, or draws. Ask them to record at least two trials from starting position to promotion or to a drawn position. Each pair of students needs a set and a board, and pencils and paper for writing algebraic notation.

Expected Time

20 minutes. 5 minutes for supplies. 2 minutes for giving the introduction to the problem. 10 minutes for solving the problem and writing the solution in algebraic notation. 3 minutes for reviewing the solution with the class.

White to move

Play out position until promotion

Figure 3.6.
Whichever side moves first wins.

Evaluation

Ask a pair of students to either share their solution at the demonstration board or to read it aloud. Then tell students that whichever side moves first should win, and that the Turk insisted on moving first. That is, if white is to move then white should win. Then, if the correct solution has not yet been given, present the solution from Appendix A.

Lesson 10: Federal Sets

Objectives

Students construct a set that portrays officials currently serving in the U.S. House of Representatives and the U.S. Senate on the white side. On the black side, the set represents the Executive Branch. Students learn the titles of legislative and executive branch leaders.

NCSS Theme

VI. Power, Authority, & Governance.

Materials and Sources

Web sites listing current U.S. representatives, senators, the 15 executive department heads (Cabinet members), the Vice President, and the President. For the Congressional leadership, I used the Web sites http://www.senate. gov/pagelayout/senators/a_three_sections_with_teasers/leadership.htm, and http://www.house.gov/house/orgs_pub_hse_ldr_www.shtml. For the Cabinet, I used the Web site http://www.whitehouse.gov/administration/cabinet/. Copies of Figure 3.7 for half of the class, and copies of Figure 3.8 for the other half of the class. Optional: Demonstration board.

Procedure

Ask students to name the three branches of the federal government, the legislative, judicial, and executive. All three have different powers, which you should briefly review with students. Congress, the legislative branch, makes the laws. The Supreme Court, the judiciary branch, hears cases that challenge the constitutionality of laws. The President can veto laws and also enforces laws.

Chess is an imperfect model of the three-part government system, because it has only two sides. Nonetheless, designing a set with members of the legislative branch on the white side and members of the executive branch on the black side will help students remember those leaders. Depending on how many students you have, have each student find out the names of one or more current governmental leaders listed for white on Figure 3.7 or for black on Figure 3.8. Give students time on the Internet, at school or as homework, to research.

If more time is available for the white side, have students research the powers and duties of the various representatives and senators. Then students may debate among themselves about which elected officials should be represented as higher-value pieces. After students assign pieces, the remaining important officials should be assigned center (e- and d-) pawns, and less important officials assigned rook (a- and h-) pawns. Whether students' research found the powers and duties or just officeholders' names, the students assigned to white-side government officials sit together to complete Figure 3.7.

Directions: This worksheet is about federal government officials, who meet in Washington, D.C. The king of the white pieces (legislative branch) is the Vice President, who serves as the nonvoting President of the Senate. The 15 other white chessmen are some of the leaders of Congress. In consultation with the other white-side students, decide where to write Congressional titles and names in the chart below.

From the House of Representatives, 5 chessmen: the Speaker of the House, the Majority Leader, the Minority Leader, the Majority Whip, and the Minority Whip.

From the Senate, 10 chessmen: President Pro Tempore, Majority Leader, Assistant Majority Leader, Minority Leader, Assistant Minority Leader, Democratic Conference Secretary, Republican Conference Secretary, and Republican Conference Chair. (No separate chessman represents the Democratic Conference Chair, since the Democratic Leader serves as Chair too.) Find out the names of your state's senators, for two more chessmen. If your state senator holds a Senate leadership position, then he or she gets to be two different chessmen.

Symbol	Title	Name of Current Office Holder
♔	Vice President (President of the Senate)	
♕		
♖ a1		
♖ h1		
♗ c1		
♗ f1		
♘ b1		
♘ g1		
♙ a2		
♙ b2		
♙ c2		
♙ d2		
♙ e2		
♙ f2		
♙ g2		
♙ h2		

Figure 3.7.
White pieces: Legislative branch.

Name_____

Directions: This worksheet is about federal government officials, who meet in Washington, DC. The President is the king of the black pieces (executive branch) and the heads of 15 executive departments, all members of the Cabinet, are the other black chessmen. In consultation with the other black-side students, choose where to write Cabinet titles and names in the chart below. There are 14 Secretaries in the Cabinet: Agriculture, Commerce, Defense, Education, Energy, Health and Human Services, Homeland Security, Housing and Urban Development, Interior, Labor, State, Transportation, Treasury, and Veterans Affairs. For each, write "Secretary of Name of Department," for example Secretary of Agriculture. A fifteenth Cabinet member is the Attorney General.

The Cabinet also includes the Vice President, but the Vice President is listed with the white pieces (legislative branch) as the President of the Senate.

Symbol	Title	Name of Current Office Holder
♚	President	
♛		
♜ a8		
♜ h8		
♝ c8		
♝ f8		
♞ b8		
♞ g8		
♟ a7		
♟ b7		
♟ c7		
♟ d7		
♟ e7		
♟ f7		
♟ g7		
♟ h7		

Figure 3.8.
Black pieces: Executive branch.

From *People, Places, Checkmates: Teaching Social Studies with Chess* by Alexey W. Root. Santa Barbara, CA: Libraries Unlimited. Copyright © 2010.

On the black side, if more time is available, have students research the duties of each Cabinet member. Then students may debate among themselves about which Cabinet members should be represented as higher-value pieces. After all pieces are assigned, remaining important officials should be assigned center (e- and d-) pawns, and less important officials assigned rook (a- and h-) pawns. The black side should likewise sit together to complete Figure 3.8.

Evaluation

Correct figures 3.7 and 3.8. Answers will vary based on the year completed, because office holders change. In Appendix A are answers from October 2009. My ranking of the chessmen/officeholders is not definitive. Indeed, if the optional extra research was conducted, ask each side (white and black) why they assigned certain governmental leaders to certain chessmen.

If there is time in class, and if students are chess players, have the white side challenge the black side to a chess game. After consulting with his or her side, the white-side spokesperson announces a move. The move should be played on the demonstration board for the black side to consider. The title and name of the chessman should be announced too, for example, 1. e4, Our House Republican Whip Eric Cantor moves to e4. Then the black side considers its move and announces it through its spokesperson, and so forth.

SMS chess advisory students' homework was to use the Internet to research the white-side and black-side officials. Each student had been assigned to find out the names of two political officeholders. When it came time to play the game on the demonstration board, if a side did not have a political leader's name for a chessman, then that side had to play without that chessman. As it turned out, each side had researched enough names to label eight chessmen. So the demonstration board game was white pieces versus black pieces, with no pawns.

Exercise 10: Thomas Jefferson

Teacher Background

On December 4, 1801, after several months of living in the White House (then called the Presidential Mansion), President Thomas Jefferson requested, "I will pray you at the same time to send me Philidor on chess, which you will find in the book room" (Onuf, n.d.). François-André Danican Philidor's *Analysis of the Game of Chess* was first published in French in 1749. Instantly popular, the book went through many editions and was translated into several languages including English.

Procedure and Materials

Tell students that they will be practicing an endgame, from François-André Danican Philidor's *Analysis of the Game of Chess,* that was likely studied by the third President of the United States, Thomas Jefferson. Philidor (1726–1795) was the world's best chess player in the mid-18th century. He was also a composer of operas. Philidor wrote in French, but Jefferson may have read an English edition of the book. Before the late 20th century, **descriptive notation** was used. Read or display the Philidor quote below on an overhead, then ask your students to determine the starting position of the chessmen and the first move of the endgame:

Situation of the White.

> The K. at the adverse K. B. fourth square.
> The P. at its K. fourth square.
> The R. at the adverse K. R. second square.

Situation of the Black.

> The K. at his home.
> The R. at its Q. R. third square.

1.

> *Wh.* The P. one move.
> *Bl.* The R. at its Q. Kt. third square. (Philidor,1749/1790, p. 91; italics in the original)

Call on different students to translate, from descriptive to algebraic notation, each line of Philidor. After the students' translation, read this paragraph aloud. The white king at its adversary's king's bishop's fourth square would be Kf5. To locate some of the other chessmen, count from one's own side. For example, the black rook at its own queen's rook's third square (counting from black's side) would translate to Ra6. The first moves are 1. e5 Rb6.

Use a demonstration board or dry-erase board to display Figure 3.9. If using a dry erase board, write, White: Kf5; Rh7; Pe4. Black: Ke8; Ra6. White to move. According to the Philidor excerpt, the first moves are 1. e5 Rb6, and then students may choose what to do. Ask students to vote whether they think that white can win or only draw with best play by both sides.

Pass out a set and board, and pencils and paper for writing algebraic notation, to each pair of students. Tell students to play 1. e5 Rb6, and to take turns playing white. Ask each student to notate one attempt to win as white and one attempt to draw as black.

White to move

Play continues 1. e5 Rb6

Figure 3.9.
A Philidor's Position.

Expected Time

25 minutes. 5 minutes for supplies. 5 minutes for giving the introduction to the problem. 10 minutes for attempting the position and writing algebraic notation. 5 minutes for reviewing the

solution with the class. As noted in the evaluation section, the time for reviewing the solution ideally should be expanded, giving students the opportunity to retry the endgame after learning its pattern.

Evaluation

Chances are that students will not figure out the drawing method unless they have previously studied this endgame. Therefore, show the correct procedure. Share Philidor's note on the correctness of the initial black move. Philidor (1749/1790, p. 91) wrote, "By keeping that line with his Rook, he hinders your King from advancing; and if he were to desert that line before you had pushed your Pawn, he would lose the game."

In other words, black needs to keep his rook on the sixth rank, to prevent the white king from advancing. But after the pawn advances to the sixth rank, the black rook moves to the first or second rank (white's side of the board) and gives **perpetual check** to the white king. Or the black rook exchanges itself for the white rook to achieve a drawn king and pawn ending. This Philidor's position, with correct play, is a draw. Show the solution from Appendix A on the demonstration board. If another 25 minutes is available, students might practice the correct ideas for this endgame with sets and boards.

Chapter 4

CHESS AND CITIZENSHIP

The lessons in chapter 4 may be taught in any order. In lesson 11, students apply *The Morals of Chess* by Benjamin Franklin. For lesson 12, students recognize famous chess players. In lesson 13, students learn about chess philanthropy by GM Yury Shulman's organization "Chess Without Borders." For lesson 14, students comprehend the criteria for college chess scholarships. In lesson 15, students debate participation guidelines for chess-playing immigrants to the United States.

Lesson 11: Benjamin Franklin

Objectives

Students list undesirable behaviors that sometimes occur during modern chess games. Through reading a primary source, students learn that Benjamin Franklin faced similar problems.

NCSS Theme

I. Culture.

Materials and Sources

Franklin (1779/1987) is a 15-paragraph essay. For this lesson, students read 9 paragraphs about proper chess behavior. Figure 4.1 contains those paragraphs, plus questions about the reading. Make one copy of

Name_____

DIRECTIONS: Read the excerpt from *The Morals of Chess* by Benjamin Franklin. The spelling and punctuation have been retained from Franklin's original document. Then answer part I (eight matching questions) and Part II (two short answers) below.

That we may, therefore, be induced more frequently to chuse this beneficial amusement, in preference to others which are not attended with the same advantages, every Circumstance, that may increase the pleasure of it should be regarded; and every action or word that is unfair, disrespectful, or that in any way may give uneasiness, should be avoided, as contrary to the immediate intention of both the Players, which is to pass the Time agreeably.

Therefore, first, if it is agreed to play according to the strict rules, then those rules are to be exactly observed by both parties, and should not be insisted on for one side, while deviated from by the other—for this is not equitable.

Secondly, if it is agreed not to observe the rules exactly, but one party demands indulgencies, he should then be as willing to allow them to the other.

Thirdly, no false move should ever be made to extricate yourself out of a difficulty, or to gain an advantage. There can be no pleasure in playing with a person once detected in such unfair practice.

Fourthly, if your adversary is long in playing, you ought not to hurry him, or express any uneasiness at his delay. You should not sing, nor whistle, nor look at your watch, nor take up a book to read, nor make a tapping with your feet on the floor, or with your fingers on the table, nor do anything that may disturb his attention. For all these things displease; and they do not show your skill in playing, but your craftiness or your rudeness.

Fifthly, you ought not to endeavour to amuse and deceive your adversary, by pretending to have made bad moves, and saying you have now lost the game, in order to make him secure and careless, and inattentive to your schemes: for this is fraud and deceit, not skill in the game.

Sixthly, you must not, when you have gained a victory, use any triumphing or insulting expression, nor show too much pleasure; but endeavour to console your adversary, and make him less dissatisfied with himself, by every kind of civil expression, that may be used with truth, such as, "you understand the game better than I, but you are a little inattentive;" or, "you play too fast;" or, "you had the best of the game, but something happened to divert your thoughts, and that turned it in my favour."

Seventhly, if you are a spectator, while others play, observe the most perfect silence. For, if you give advice, you offend both parties; him, against whom you give it, because it may cause the loss of his game, him, in whose favour you give it, because, though it be good, and he follows it, he loses the pleasure he might have had, if you had permitted him to think until it had occurred to himself. Even after a move or moves, you must not, by replacing the pieces, show how they might have been placed better; for that displeases, and may occasion disputes and doubts about their true situation. All talking to the players lessens or diverts their attention, and is therefore unpleasing. Nor should you give the least hint to either party, by any kind of noise or motion. If you do, you are unworthy to be a spectator. If you have a mind to exercise or show your judgments, do it in playing your own game, when you have an opportunity, not in criticizing, or meddling with, or counselling the play of others.

Lastly, if the game is not to be played rigorously, according to the rules above mentioned, then moderate your desire of victory over your adversary, and be pleased with one over yourself. Snatch not eagerly at every advantage offered by his unskilfulness or inattention; but point out to him kindly, that by such a move he places or leaves a piece in danger and unsupported; that by another he will put his king in a perilous situation, &c. By this generous civility (so opposite to the unfairness above

Figure 4.1.
The Morals of Chess worksheet.

forbidden) you may, indeed, happen to lose the game to your opponent; but you will win what is better, his esteem, his respect, and his affection; together with the silent approbation and good-will of impartial spectators.

I. Mark with an X the behaviors that were mentioned in Benjamin Franklin's *The Morals of Chess*.

_____1. Cheating (making false moves)

_____2. Giving your adversary a big meal to cloud his thinking

_____3. Giving advice as a spectator

_____4. Rushing your adversary by tapping your feet

_____5. Hurrying your adversary by singing

_____6. Placing the board so that the sun is in your adversary's eyes

_____7. Pretending to make a bad move to trick your adversary

_____8. Following the rules exactly by one side, but the other side not following the rules

_____9. Winning a game, and then making an insulting expression

II. Of the behaviors that you marked with an X in part I, pick one that have you encountered (or heard about) in a chess game in modern times. Answer A. and B. on notebook paper, writing one paragraph for A. and writing two paragraphs for B.

A. Name the behavior and tell when or where the behavior occurred.

B. What could be done to minimize that behavior, first according to Franklin and then according to you?

Figure 4.1.
(continued).

From *People, Places, Checkmates: Teaching Social Studies with Chess* by Alexey W. Root. Santa Barbara, CA: Libraries Unlimited. Copyright © 2010.

Figure 4.1 for each student. In addition to their copies of Figure 4.1, students need pens or pencils and notebook paper.

Procedure

Ask students what behaviors need correction during chess games, either within their class or when they play outside of school. Students might mention gloating after wins, distracting (through talking, foot tapping, etc.), gambling (or saying "I bet I can beat you"), and not following the **touch move** rule.

If students cannot generate tales share news media or personal stories. One of Anna Rudolf's opponents at the Vandoeuvre Open, December 2007, refused her handshake. That opponent believed that Anna had cheated by having a computer in her lip balm; see http://interviews. chessdom.com/anna-rudolf. My personal story is that I pointed out moves to players contesting nonladder games. The one whose turn it was might not have seen my suggested move. Thus my advice may have changed the course of the game. Or my suggested move annoyed the player by revealing what he or she had planned. The chess term for my behavior is **kibitzing.** Complaints from my students may have cured me of this habit.

Write the problematic behaviors on the board. Tell students that Benjamin Franklin faced some of these same challenges over 200 years ago. He wrote *The Morals of Chess* "with a view to correct (among a few young friends) some little improprieties in the practice of" chess (1779/1987, p. 928). Ask students to read the last nine paragraphs of Franklin's essay (pp. 929–931), starting with the phrase "that we may therefore be induced more frequently to chuse [choose] this beneficial amusement" of chess. Those paragraphs, and related questions for students to answer, are on Figure 4.1.

Evaluation

The answer key for Figure 4.1 is in Appendix A. The incorrect answers (numbers 2 and 6) derive from older sources than Franklin. According to Pandolfini (2007, p. 181), the advice to play soon after your opponent has eaten and drunk freely is from Luis Ramirez de Lucena of Spain (1465–1530). The advice to place the board so that the sun is in your opponent's eyes is from the 16th-century Spanish chess writer, player, and clergyman Ruy Lopez (Pandolfini, p. 182). Ask students if Franklin would have recommended either of these tactics. Answer: No, because he thought that treating the opponent with respect was more important than winning.

Read the students' short answers from part II of Figure 4.1. If they point to behaviors that should be corrected, reevaluate classroom chess procedures. Appendix A has part II answers from three of my SMS chess advisory students.

Exercise 11: Bughouse

Teacher Background

Figure 4.2 provides rules for bughouse. Once students learn bughouse, they often choose to play during any free time available. On character education and study skills days, after finishing their lesson with Mr. Mc-Clanahan, students sometimes played bughouse. Similarly, at the holiday chess party, several students played bughouse.

Optional: type the search string "bughouse chess rules" to find Web sites for the rules of bughouse. You can play bughouse on several online chess servers. For three bughouse essays that I co-authored see Root and Wiggins (2003).

Procedure and Materials

Explain the role of clocks in bughouse, and how to play without clocks. Bughouse requires two sets and two boards for every four students. Chess clocks inhibit stalling, the term for waiting for an important piece. For example, sometimes an additional queen would allow a player to checkmate. Therefore, stalling (waiting) to get that queen wins the game. But with clocks set at five minutes per side, excessive stalling fails because a loss on time means a loss of the game.

Without clocks, theoretically someone could stall forever. When I taught bughouse without clocks during 2007–2008, I initially insisted on a strict order for bughouse. Both white players moved. Then the blacks moved. Then the whites moved, and so on. By this pattern of alternating, one team could not stall. Though my rules prevented stalling, students complained that the alternating made bughouse boring and slow. So they voluntarily agreed not to stall for material, and bughouse became exciting and fun. Ask students what bughouse rules Benjamin Franklin might suggest.

Put Figure 4.2 on the overhead projector, or make copies for each two-person bughouse team. Figure 4.2 requests that students forgo stalling and show respect, just as Benjamin Franklin asked for good chess behavior. Bughouse requires even more politeness than regular chess, because you have more people (your own partner, plus two people on the opposing team) to consider. State that you will be observing games with pen and notepad, and writing down which players are polite to their partners and opponents. Then assign (or let students choose) partners, pass out sets and boards (and clocks if available), and allow students to play bughouse for the remainder of the period.

Expected Time

25 minutes. 5 minutes for supplies. 5 minutes for discussion of clocks, Franklin-style bughouse rules, and Figure 4.2. 14 minutes for playing bughouse. 1 minute for evaluation.

1. Bughouse is a chess variant played with two boards and four players. Two players sit next to each other, one on each board, and are called partners or a bughouse team. The other two players sit across from the first team, and are the other team.

2. The main difference from regular chess is that, in bughouse, chessmen captured on your partner's board can be placed on your board.

3. You will play the opposite color from your partner. That is, if your partner plays black on his or her board, you will play white on your board. Your partner captures white chessmen and hands them to you.

4. On your turn, you may move your chessmen already on your board or drop (insert, place) a chessman given to you on any open square. You can drop in checks and checkmates. EXCEPTION: You may not drop a pawn handed to you on your first or eighth rank.

5. If a pawn promotes, announce what it has promoted to then lay the pawn on its side. It will function as the promoted piece until it is captured. Then it reverts to being a pawn.

6. The opposing team must be able to see all the pieces and pawns that you have available for dropping into the game.

7. Because of the symbiotic relationship between bughouse partners, bughouse is sometimes called Siamese chess. For this reason, treat your partner as you wish to be treated. You cannot touch your partner's board or chessmen, but you can advise using notation. For example, you might say, "Protect your f7 by dropping a pawn there." If your partner hands you a chessman, say thank you. If you need a chessman, say please.

8. Treat the other team respectfully. If playing without chess clocks, this means no stalling. Please do not take longer on a move (than you otherwise would) to wait for material that would allow you to checkmate.

9. Without clocks, taking your hand off the chessman that you have moved or dropped on the board means that your move is done. With clocks, your move is complete when you punch your clock. You can take kings to win, and (with clocks) you can win on time.

10. If one member of a team wins, the whole team wins.

Figure 4.2.
Rules for bughouse.

Evaluation

As students are playing bughouse, walk around with a notepad and pen. Take notes on polite and impolite behaviors. Since students know what you are doing, just seeing you with your notepad will remind them to be polite. If behaviors were in line with Figure 4.2, at dismissal give this quick compliment, "Benjamin Franklin would be proud of the way you interacted with your partner and opponents!"

Lesson 12: Famous Chess Players

Objectives

Students memorize facts about 10 famous chess players. Students use factors such as capabilities, motivation, personality, and behavior to identify which player is being described.

NCSS Theme

IV. Individual Development & Identity.

Materials and Sources

This lesson requires one blank stick-on name tag per student. On each blank name tag, write the bold italic information listed for one player in Figure 4.3: *name of the player* and *tagline about that player*. One photocopy of Figure 4.3 for each student. Optional: For evaluation, make one copy of Figure 4.4, a quiz, for each student.

I borrowed this activity from my son William's SMS theater teacher Susie Norton. In her November 6, 2008 class, students wore name tags of pretend superheroes on their backs. Then they asked yes or no questions to deduce their superhero identity. William's tag read "Chess Man: Strategist of highest power." I asked William how he figured out what superhero he was. He said his first clue was when he got a "yes" answer to his question "Am I smart?"

To create Figure 4.3, I chose Internet sites that were written or authorized by the famous player, or sites that had content verified by other sources. I listed those sites at the end of each minibiography. You may search the Internet for images of the famous players to show to your students. Figure 4.5 is a photo of Viswanathan Anand and Figure 4.6 is a photo of Judit Polgár.

If there are more than 10 students in your room, some students will have identical name tags. That is, there might be two or three students with the "*Maurice Ashley. First African American to attain the GM title*" name tag.

Procedure

Pass out copies of Figure 4.3. Tell your students that memorizing most of the information in Figure 4.3's biographies is crucial to their success. Within seven minutes, most will have memorized at least part

Listed below are 10 famous chess players. After the name is a tagline to help you remember the player. Both the player's name and his or her tagline are ***bold italic***. Then other information is listed: The dates in parentheses are the (birth date–date of death). GM stands for Grandmaster, the highest title in chess aside from World Champion. Listed at the end of each paragraph is the Web site source of the biographical information.

Viswanathan Anand. First World Champion from India. (1969–). Also known by the nickname Vishy, Anand was India's first GM. As of this writing (2009), he reigns as the World Champion of chess. He is a national hero in India, having received sportsperson of the year awards and an honorary doctorate. Personable and friendly, Anand is known for playing accurately and rapidly. http://www.tnq.in/vishwa.html

Maurice Ashley. First African American to Attain the GM Title. (1966–). Ashley became the first African American to earn the GM title in 1999. He also is famous as a chess teacher. He coached a team from Harlem, the Raging Rooks, who tied for first in the National Junior High Championship in 1991. GM Ashley has received multiple community service awards from city governments, universities, and nonprofit groups for his work. *Chess for Success* (Ashley, 2005) crystallizes his vision of using chess to help at-risk youth. Ashley is an ESPN commentator on chess matches, giving comments much like a sportscaster does for athletic events. http://www.mauriceashley.com/

José Raúl Capablanca. World Champion from Cuba. (1888–1942). Capablanca was a GM from Cuba who was World Champion from 1921 to 1927. From 1914–1924 he lost only one game. In addition to playing chess, he also acted in a movie, "Chess Fever," attended Columbia University, worked for the Cuban Foreign Office, and wrote chess books. His *Chess Fundamentals* is a classic instructional book. http://www.chesscorner.com/worldchamps/capablanca/capablanca.htm

Bobby Fischer. World Champion from the United States. (1943–2008). In the summer of 1972, GM Fischer defeated World Champion Boris Spassky by a score of 12.5–8.5. Fischer became the first—and as yet the only—American to win the title of World Champion. Fischer said, "Chess is war over the board. The object is to crush the opponent's mind." In 1974, Fischer did not defend his championship title. For the remainder of his life, he lived as a recluse. Fischer stated that the September 11, 2001 attack on the United States was "wonderful news." http://www.nytimes.com/2008/01/18/obituaries/18cnd-fischer.html

Garry Kasparov. World Champion versus Computer. (1963–). GM Garry Kasparov was the top-ranked player in the world from 1984 to 2005 and World Champion from 1985 to 2000. He played two widely publicized matches against the IBM computer Deep Blue, winning in 2006 and losing in 2007. He chairs the Kasparov Chess Foundation, which developed a K–12 chess curriculum. Kasparov wrote on the foundation's Web site, http://www.kasparovchessfoundation.org/, "We've designed a program that encourages creativity, instills self-discipline and offers hope and a feeling of accomplishment to millions of children." Kasparov is a political force for democracy in Russia. http://www.kasparovagent.com/garry_kasparov_biography.php

Paul Morphy. The Pride and Sorrow of Chess. (1837–1884). Morphy was a chess prodigy, but then he turned his attention to school. Morphy was an excellent student, finishing law school at age 19. Still too young to practice law, Morphy returned to chess and won the U.S. Chess Championship at the age of 20. He then proceeded to Europe to defeat the best players there, except for English champion Howard Staunton (who avoided a match with Morphy). Though the title of World Champion had not yet been established, many consider Morphy an unofficial World Champion. Morphy returned to the United States and intended to be a lawyer. Morphy opposed the secession of Louisiana from the Union and subsequently was unable to get clients for his law practice. He died without a legal or chess career. http://www.jeremysilman.com/chess_history/grt_plyr_pc_morphy.html

Figure 4.3.
Chess biographies.

Judit Polgár. Best Woman Chess Player of the 20th Century. (1976–). Quoting Judit,

Practically from the moment of my birth, on July 23, 1976, I became involved in an educational experiment. Even before I came into the world, my parents had already decided: I would be a chess player. My sister Susan had been a successful player for years, winning one tournament after the other. Based on educational research, our parents decided that their children's lives and careers would be a living example that would prove that any healthy child—if taught early and intensively—can be brought up to be an outstanding person—or, in the words of my father László Polgár: a genius. . . .

In 1991, I became Chess Grandmaster, breaking Bobby Fischer's record as youngest grandmaster in history at the time. On four occasions, I played on the Hungarian men's Olympic chess team, and we won a silver medal in 2002. I have defeated world chess champions Spassky, Karpov, Kasparov, Topalov and Anand at international tournaments, matches and rapid tournaments.

I have been the world's No. 1 woman chess player for nearly 20 years straight, since 1989. Among men, I was ranked 8th in 2005.

http://www.polgarjudit.com/biography_en.html (quote downloaded November 21, 2008)

Yury Shulman, U.S. Champion and MBA. (1975–). Born in Belarus, GM Shulman came to the United States on a chess scholarship from The University of Texas at Dallas (UTD). GM Shulman played first board and served as team captain for the UTD chess team. He also earned a bachelor's degree and a master's in business administration (MBA). He now runs the Yury Shulman International Chess School and is on the board of directors for Chess Without Borders (see Lesson Thirteen). http://www.shulmanchess.com/

Wilhelm (William) Steinitz. First Official World Champion. (1836–1900). Born in Prague (now in the Czech Republic), Steinitz became a strong chess player in Austria. From 1872 to 1882, he did not play much but developed theories about chess that were the basis for his articles and books. He moved to the United States in 1882. In 1886, he won a match against Johannes Zukertort to become World Chess Champion. The match was played in three cities in the United States: New York, St. Louis, and New Orleans. Although Steinitz earned money from tournaments and matches, it was not enough. Also, he was a poor money manager. He died penniless. http://www.chesscorner.com/worldchamps/steinitz/steinitz.htm

Josh Waitzkin, Champion in Chess and Martial Arts. (1976–). Josh Waitzkin learned chess at six, began studying with Bruce Pandolfini at seven, and dominated scholastic tournaments from age nine through high school. Fred Waitzkin (Josh's father) wrote *Searching for Bobby Fischer* about Josh's early chess years. The book became an Academy Award–nominated film. After earning the International Master title in chess, Josh competed in Tai Chi and is a two-time Middleweight World Champion in Fixed Step Push Hands. He coached chess, created chess software, and founded an educational nonprofit, The JW Foundation. http://www.joshwaitzkin.com/

Figure 4.3.
(continued).

From *People, Places, Checkmates: Teaching Social Studies with Chess* by Alexey W. Root. Santa Barbara, CA: Libraries Unlimited. Copyright © 2010.

Name_____

Match the names of 10 famous chess players (1–10) with their biographies (a–j). The players are listed alphabetically by last name on the top half of this worksheet. The biographies are listed below all the names. Put the letter of the correct biography next to the number of the player that it describes.

_____1. Viswanathan Anand

_____2. Maurice Ashley

_____3. José Raúl Capablanca

_____4. Bobby Fischer

_____5. Garry Kasparov

_____6. Paul Morphy

_____7. Judit Polgár

_____8. Yury Shulman

_____9. Wilhelm Steinitz

_____10. Josh Waitzkin

a. *First African American to Attain the GM Title.* He is an ESPN commentator on chess matches, giving comments much like a sportscaster does for athletic events.

b. *First Official World Champion.* In 1886, he won a match against Johannes Zukertort to become World Chess Champion.

c. *Best Woman Chess Player of the 20th Century.* As of 2009, she has been the world's top woman chess player for 20 years and was ranked as high as eighth best player in the world (men and women combined rating list) in 2005.

d. *First World Champion from India.* He is a national hero in India, receiving sportsperson of the year awards and an honorary doctorate.

e. *The Pride and Sorrow of Chess.* He went to Europe to defeat the best players there before returning to his native Louisiana.

f. *World Champion versus Computer.* The top-ranked player in the world from 1984 to 2005 and World Champion from 1985 to 2000. He played two widely publicized matches against the IBM computer Deep Blue, winning in 2006 and losing in 2007.

g. *World Champion from Cuba.* From 1914 to 1924 he lost only one game. His *Chess Fundamentals* is a classic instructional book.

h. *World Champion from the United States.* The first—and as yet the only—American to win the title of World Champion in 1972.

i. *U.S. Champion and MBA.* A Grandmaster and U.S. Champion, he teaches chess and practices philanthropy.

j. *Champion in Chess and Martial Arts.* An International Master whose scholastic chess tournament successes became the subject of a book and motion picture.

Figure 4.4.
Biography quiz.

From *People, Places, Checkmates: Teaching Social Studies with Chess* by Alexey W. Root. Santa Barbara, CA: Libraries Unlimited. Copyright © 2010.

Figure 4.5.
Viswanathan Anand.

Figure 4.6.
Judit Polgár.

of Figure 4.3. Then ask students to put Figure 4.3 out of sight, for example in their notebooks or face down.

Call each student to the front of the room and put a name tag on his or her back. That is, the name tag must be invisible to the tagged student. Once all students have been tagged, they will walk around the room asking each other yes or no questions to figure out their identities. I compared their walking around to a party for amnesiac living and dead chess players, all of whom want to find out who they are. Tagged students cannot ask if they have a particular name. They may ask, "Am I dead?" or "Am I female?" After giving these instructions, let them begin the "amnesiac party."

When ready to guess their names, students approach the teacher. If a student correctly says the name on his or her back, the teacher removes the tag. Students who have guessed correctly may still answer yes or no questions. Or they may prepare for evaluation by studying Figure 4.3.

Evaluation

One level of evaluation would be to watch the students during the name tag exercise. Was each student able to figure out his or her identity? A second evaluation would be to revise Figure 4.3 into a quiz. One such quiz is Figure 4.4, and the answer key is in Appendix A.

Here are some options for extending lesson 12. If your library has chess books or magazines, or you can bookmark reliable Internet sites, ask each student to write a paper about the famous player on his or her name tag. You might also give students more than 10 choices for biographical research by listing additional famous players.

Exercise 12: Famous Chess Moves

Teacher Background

One option is to search for games online using the terms "chess game database." Or simply use the positions in Figure 4.7, compiled with the help of my husband IM Doug Root and my Chess in Education Certificate Online student WFM Chouchanik Airapetian.

Positions in Figure 4.7 have tactical solutions between two and seven moves long. In other words, the positions are challenging for intermediate

Positions and Solutions for *Exercise 12: Famous Chess Moves*. Player with white is listed first. The player profiled in Lesson 12 is listed in ***bold italic***. Find a winning line for the side that is to move in each position below.

Position	Solution
Vladimir Kramnik vs. ***Anand***, Game 3, 2008 World Chess Championship Match. White: Ka2; Ra3; P's a7, b2, f4, f3, h2. Black: Kh6; Qf1; Bf5; P's e6, f6, h5. Black to move.	Kramnik vs. Anand: 1....Bb1+ and white resigned. But two possible lines are 2. Ka1 Bc2+ 3. Ka2 Qb1# Or 1....Bb1+ 2. Kb3 Qxf3+ with the idea of Qa8 to stop white's a-pawn. Then black is ahead enough material to win.
Ashley vs. Josh Waitzkin, Mermaid Beach Club, Bermuda, 1997. White: Kh1; Qf3; R's f1, d2; P's a2, c2, e4, g2, h2. Black: Kc7; Qc5; R's c8, g8; Bd7; P's a7, e5, h7. White to move.	Ashley vs. Waitzkin: 1. Rxd7+ Kxd7 2. Qf7+ Kc6 3. Rf6+ Kb5 4. Qb7+ Qb6 (if 4....Ka4 5. Ra6+ Qa5 6. Qb3#) 5. Rxb6 axb6 and white has an advantage. White won after 40 more moves.

Position	Solution
Capablanca vs. David Janowski, Round 6, Manhattan (NY) Chess Club Masters, 1918. White: Kg1; Qh5; R's d4, g6; Bc4; P's b2, e3, f2, g2, h2. Black: Kh8; Qc5; R's d8, f8; Nb4; P's a7, f5, h7. White to move.	Capablanca vs. Janowski: 1. Rg7 and black resigned because of 1....Kxg7 2.Qg5+ Kh8 3.Rxd8 then 3....Rxd8 is not possible because of 4. Qf6#. If 3....Nd5 4. Rxf8+ Qxf8 5. Bxd5.
Arinbjorn Gudmundsson vs. ***Fischer***, Reykjavik, Iceland, 1960. White: Kg3; B's b1, d2; P's a2, c3, f4, g2, h3. Black: Kg8; Re8; P's a7, b7, c6, f5, f7, h7. Black to move.	Gudmundsson vs. Fischer: 1....Re2 and white resigned because of 2. Bc1 Re1 wins one of white's bishops.
Michael Adams vs. ***Kasparov***, Linares, 2005. White: Ka2; Qd2; R's g1, h1; B's e2, g5; Na4; P's b2, e4, f3, h5. Black: Kh7; Qc5; R's b8, f8; B's a8, e5; Na3; P's a6, d6, e6, f7, g7. Black to move.	Adams vs. Kasparov: 1....Nc2 and if 2. Nxc5 Rxb2#. Adams played 2. Kb1 Qa3 and Adams resigned because of 3. Qxc2 Rfc8 4. Qd2 Qxa4 with the threat of....Rxb2+.

Figure 4.7.
Positions and solutions.

From *People, Places, Checkmates: Teaching Social Studies with Chess* by Alexey W. Root. Santa Barbara, CA: Libraries Unlimited. Copyright © 2010.

Position	Solution
Morphy vs. team of Duke of Brunswick and Count of Isouard, Paris Opera House, 1858. White: Kc1; Qb3; Rd1; Bg5; P's a2, b2, c2, e4, f2, g2, h2. Black: Ke8; Qe6; Rh8; Bf8; Nd7; P's a7, e5, f7, g7, h7. White to move.	Morphy vs. consultation team: 1. Qb8+ Nxb8 2. Rd8#.
Polgár vs. Ferenc Berkes, Hunguest Hotels Super Chess Tournament, Budapest, 2003. White: Kc1; Qf4; R's d1, h1; Be4; Nf3; P's a2, b2, c2, d4, f2, g4, g5. Black: Kg7; Qd8; R's b8, f8; B's e7, b7; Nd7; P's a7, b6, c7, e6, f7, g6. White to move.	Polgár vs. Berkes: 1. Rh7+. The game continued 1.... Kxh7 2. Qh2+ Kg8 (if instead 2....Kg7 3. Qh6+ with the idea of Rh1 as in the game) 3. Rh1 Bxg5+ (Forced move for black, because white threatens Qh7# and Qh8#). 4. Nxg5 Qxg5+ 5. f4 Qxf4+ 6. Qxf4 Bxe4 7. Qxe4 and black resigned.
Josh Friedel vs. *Shulman*, United States Chess Championship, St. Louis, 2009. White: Kf1; Re6; Bh4; Nc4; Ps a3, h2. Black: Kg8; Rg4; Be4; P's g7, g6, h6. Black to move.	Friedel vs. Shulman: 1....Bd3+ and white resigned because of 2. Kf2 Bxc4 3. Re8+ Kf7 4. Re7+ Kf8 and the bishop on h4 will be captured by black's rook.
Steinitz vs. Mikhail Chigorin, Havana, Game 4, 1892 World Chess Championship Match. White: Kc1; Qh1; B's b3, h6; P's a2, b2, c3, f2, g2. Black: Kf6; Qc6; R's e8, f8; Bd7; Nd4; P's a5, b7, c7, g6. White to move.	Steinitz vs. Chigorin: 1. Qh4+ Ke5 2. Qxd4+ Kf5 3. Qf4#
Waitzkin vs. Larry Christiansen, Chicago, 1998. White: Kf3; Qf2; R's a1, h6; Nd7; P's b2, e4, f5, g4. Black: Kf7; Qa2; Rg7; Bb7; P's a6, b5, c2, d6, e5. White to move.	Waitzkin vs. Christiansen: 1. Nxe5+ dxe5 2. Qxc2 and black resigned because of 2....Qxa1 3. Qc7+ Kf8 4. Rh8+ Rg8 5. Qd8+ Kf7 6. Qxg8+ Ke7 7. Qe6#

Figure 4.7.
(continued).

From *People, Places, Checkmates: Teaching Social Studies with Chess* by Alexey W. Root. Santa Barbara, CA: Libraries Unlimited. Copyright © 2010.

students. Students might solve two or three of the problems. When shown each problem's solution, however, they will understand it.

Procedure and Materials

Based on their name tags from lesson 12, students are already divided into 10 groups (corresponding to the 10 famous players). Each group needs one copy of the position (left column of Figure 4.7) and the solution (right column of Figure 4.7) for its player only. For example, the Anand group will use just the Anand position (first position in left column) and the Anand solution (first solution in right column). Make enough photocopies of Figure 4.7 so that you can cut along the interior and exterior borderlines of the table to separate each position and solution. Hand each group the position corresponding to its name tag. (Do not hand out the solutions at this point.) Give each group a set and board. Students also need pencils and notebook paper or score sheets.

Inform students of the procedure for solving the problem. Groups will set up the position on the board. Then each person in the group will write in notation what they think the solution might be, by looking at the board but not yet moving the chessmen around. Then each person will take turns showing his or her solution by moving the chessmen on the board. After each person has presented, the group can move the chessmen around and debate which ideas look promising. During class, observe groups to make sure this procedure is followed.

After studying the position, including moving the pieces around for five minutes, students may raise their hands for you to give them the first move of the solution. Then the group can try solving the position again. When a group thinks it has all the moves of the solution, the group should write its answer in algebraic notation.

When groups bring you their written solutions, hand them the solutions from Figure 4.7. If their solution was different from the one in Figure 4.7, groups should play out the moves of the Figure 4.7 solution on their chess sets and boards.

Expected Time

25 minutes. 5 minutes for supplies. 2 minutes for giving the introduction to the problem. 10 minutes for solving the problem and writing the solution in algebraic notation. 8 minutes for evaluation.

Evaluation

After the procedure, each famous-player group should demonstrate its Figure 4.7 position and solution to another famous-player group. An easy way is for one name-tag group (for example, Maurice Ashley) to show the Ashley position and solution to the students who had another name tag (for example, Judit Polgár). Then the Judit Polgár students would demonstrate her position and solution to the Maurice Ashley students. Here are suggested pairings for a first round: Ashley–Polgár; Capablanca–Anand; Steinitz–Kasparov; Morphy–Fischer, and Shulman–Waitzkin. After this first round (if more sharing is desired, either during this class or in future class periods) make additional pairings.

Lesson 13: Chess Philanthropy

Objectives

Students list needs, seen either on television or in person, of people in their own city, state, nation, or world. Students identify how Chess Without Borders meets those needs.

NCSS Theme

IX. Global Connections.

Materials and Sources

One photocopy of Figure 4.8 for every student. Dr. Kiran Frey, mother of Rishi Sethi, provided a rough draft of Figure 4.8 and e-mailed the photos in Figure 4.10 and Figure A.12. *Chess Life Online* reported on philanthropy by Chess Without Borders (Dynako, 2009a; Dynako, 2009b). The Web site for Chess Without Borders is http://www.shulmanchess.com/.

Procedure

In a group discussion, students list needs in their city, state, nation, or world. Call on each student to either share a personal experience or news story, or to comment on something already said. After every student has had a chance to share, tell students that a chess organization in Barrington, Illinois, addresses some of these needs. Have them individually read and answer the questions on Figure 4.8.

Evaluation

The answer key for Figure 4.8 is in Appendix A. If students are intrigued by some of the activities undertaken by Chess Without Borders, set aside more class time to devise a chess class philanthropy project. One possible project is a **simultaneous exhibition** to raise money for charity.

Exercise 13: Simultaneous Exhibition

Teacher Background

For a simultaneous exhibition, or simul for short, arrange the available tables in an upside-down horseshoe (∩) shape or similar shape that allows the exhibitor to access its middle. Place the chairs on the outside of the horseshoe. Place the sets and boards so that the white chessmen are toward the inside of the horseshoe, and the black chessmen are nearest to

DIRECTIONS: Read the "Chess Without Borders and Philanthropy" essay. Then answer the questions at the end.

CHESS WITHOUT BORDERS AND PHILANTHROPY by Dr. Kiran Frey and Brian Gruber (the Web site for Chess Without Borders is http://www.shulmanchess.com/)

The idea of combining chess and philanthropy was born from a simple concept, that children can volunteer and accomplish things together. Rishi Sethi was nine years old when he gathered 23 elementary students to form a chess club at Grove Avenue School in Barrington, Illinois. The Grove Avenue students began teaching chess at a nursing home across the street from their school. The elderly people were lonely and bored. Learning chess gave them something to do. Also, they enjoyed meeting the elementary school students. The students liked it too. "We are all teachers," said a nine-year-old named Mark. Another student said, "It's like traveling and meeting new people."

As a result of their nursing home volunteering, the Grove Avenue students talked to reporters, collaborated with local businesses, and enrolled more volunteers. Chess clubs that combined chess and charity began at other elementary, middle, and high schools in Barrington. Rishi and his friend David, now high school students, understood what Heifer International (http://www.heifer.org/) accomplished. It donates livestock to needy families in over 50 countries (and 28 U.S. states) in order for them to become self-sufficient. So in 2003 Rishi and David organized the Heifer International Chess Tournament and thus raised $1,500 for the Heifer International charity.

In 2005, after playing chess with students at Lloyd School in Chicago, fourth-grader David Jewell learned that those students had no books at home. David became an ambassador for a book drive that collected enough books so that every Lloyd student could have at least one book at home. After realizing that the Metcalfe Elementary School library in Chicago had only a few books, elementary school ambassadors from several Barrington schools collected and then donated 2,000 books to that library.

After Grandmaster Yury Shulman moved to Barrington, he founded a K–12 organization called Chess Without Borders. His organization became the base for the elementary, middle, and high school students already deeply involved in chess and philanthropy. As Chess Without Borders is known for its philanthropy, requests are made for support. Some of these requests come from the community. For example, a community member informed the chess group that animal shelters are suffering in the current economy. In 2008, summer chess camps held at Barrington High School raised $100 for a local animal shelter. By cooperating with local businesses and nonprofit organizations such as Bertacchi Builders, Whole Foods Market, and St. Matthew Lutheran Church, Chess Without Borders donates to local or international schools and charities.

Chess students who travel to other parts of the world often take chess sets or textbooks to donate to underprivileged schools and communities. Through its Global Outreach Program, Chess Without Borders has donated chess equipment, money, and books to Nigeria, Sudan, Germany, Chile, India, Borneo, Mexico, the Dominican Republic, Malaysia, and Cambodia. Donations from Chess Without Borders established chess clubs in the Govindpura slums of Delhi and in a school for children of factory workers in India. These children have few opportunities, so establishing a chess club brings much enthusiasm and new forms of learning into their lives. Figure A.12 shows students at the school for children of factory workers in Tirupati, India enjoying one of the donated chess sets.

Although philanthropy has been going on since Rishi Sethi began the first elementary school chess club in 1998, Chess Without Borders formalized recognition of students' charity work. GM Shulman gives a Certified Chess Coach award to students who complete his book (Shulman & Sethi, 2007) and volunteer for a minimum of 20 hours. For example, student Ryan Vranek established a chess program in a nursing home as a part of earning his certificate. As of the spring of 2009, 12 students have earned this chess coach certification.

Figure 4.8.
Chess Without Borders.

From *People, Places, Checkmates: Teaching Social Studies with Chess* by Alexey W. Root. Santa Barbara, CA: Libraries Unlimited. Copyright © 2010.

Questions:

1. True or False: Elementary school students can start a chess club.

2. How did teaching chess at a nursing home benefit the elderly residents? a. they met new people b. they watched more TV c. they made money

3. Who led the collection of books for Chicago schoolchildren? a. businesses b. teachers c. elementary school students d. high school students

4. How much money was raised for Heifer International by holding a chess tournament? a. $1,000 b. $1,500 c. $2,000 d. $3,000

5. Where has Chess Without Borders donated chess equipment and books? a. Borneo b. India c. Chile d. all of the above

6. How many hours of volunteering is required as part of certification as a chess coach? a. 10 b.15 c. 20 d. 25

Figure 4.8.
(continued).

1. The exhibitor plays white on each board.

2. Bring a Staunton-style tournament chess set and board. Do not bring nonstandard or collector's chess sets.

3. Do not touch any chessman until the exhibitor arrives at your board. When the exhibitor is standing in front of your board, make your move (within 5 seconds) while the exhibitor is observing. The exhibitor will make a move on your board before going on to the next board.

4. Participants, but not the exhibitor, must abide by the touch move rule. The exhibitor's move is not final until he touches a piece on the next board.

5. Each player is allowed three passes when the exhibitor arrives at his or her board. Using a pass means that the exhibitor will skip your board, but you will need to make a move (or use another pass) when the exhibitor comes back after visiting the other boards.

6. Participants may not receive assistance from other players or bystanders during their games. Exception: participants may sign up as a pair and play on one board.

7. Participants must take notation.

8. If the exhibitor has any other rules, those will be announced at the start of the exhibition.

Figure 4.9.
Simul rules.

From *People, Places, Checkmates: Teaching Social Studies with Chess* by Alexey W. Root. Santa Barbara, CA: Libraries Unlimited. Copyright © 2010.

each chair. The giver of the simul walks around the inside of the horseshoe, making moves on each board in turn. The chairs on the outside of the simul horseshoe seat the participants, preferably one chair per board if you have enough chess equipment. If not, two students per board may team up against the exhibitor. In that case, set up two chairs per board on the outside of the horseshoe.

Decide who will be the exhibitor for the simul. If this is a warm-up for a charity simul, just to get the feel of the simul rules, the teacher might choose to act as the exhibitor. Figure 4.9 has the rules for participants in an exhibitor's simul, adapted from http://www.users.muohio.edu/brownc1/kaidanov.htm. If this is a fund-raising event, invite a strong chess player to your school.

Procedure and Materials

For a charity simul, there will be pre-event footwork: lining up the exhibitor, publicizing the event, collecting participants' fees or sponsors' donations, and so forth. Arrange the tables, chairs, sets, and boards. Then display Figure 4.9 on an overhead projector and discuss the simul rules. Ask simul participants to record their games in notation. Then begin the simul.

Expected Time

For an in-class practice simul, stop the simul after 20 minutes. A handful of games will have finished. If the simul is to be played to completion, as for a charity simul, a longer time period is needed. If the participants in the simul are rated 800 points or more below the exhibitor, a 20-game simul will take roughly two hours. Some games will finish quickly, but others will just be finishing at the two-hour mark. If there are more simul games played, or if the exhibitor and the participants are closer in strength, then the simul will take longer. Two-time U.S. Women's Chess Champion and **Woman Grandmaster (WGM)** Jennifer Shahade (Shahade, 2009) wrote:

> First up was a 26-board simul at Saint Louis's Science Center. It was one of my longest simuls ever, and certainly the longest in proportion to the number of boards. All the players were members of the Chess Club and Scholastic Center of Saint Louis, and so probably more active and sharp than in my average simul. Normally, 20–25 board simuls take me about 2.5 to three hours, while this one lasted over 4.5 hours!! I usually finish simuls more quickly because a few players drop pieces or mates early in, whereas at the Science Center, I think it took me an hour to win a pawn on any of the boards. In the end, I lost four games, won 18 and drew four.

Figure 4.10 shows Rishi Sethi, when he was a high school student, giving a simul at Metcalfe School in Chicago.

Figure 4.10.
Simultaneous exhibition.

Evaluation

Comment on students' adherence to the simul rules in Figure 4.9. Post mortems for completed games, and **adjudication** of any **adjourned** games, could occur during the next meeting time. Post-mortem guidelines are in Appendix A, Figure A.13. For adjudicating, convene a pair of students not involved in that particular game to decide which side should be given the win or if the position should be declared a draw. They should justify their adjudication by reference to the material imbalances or to the situation of one side's king.

Lesson 14: Chess Scholarships

Objectives

Students learn that universities are ranked, in part, by the quality of their student body. Students write letters that emphasize their qualities. Optional: Each student researches which university to send his or her letter to, and mails or e-mails the letter to a specific admissions counselor.

NCSS Theme

V. Individuals, Groups, & Institutions.

Materials and Sources

Dry-erase board and markers for teacher. Students need paper, and pens or pencils. Photocopy Figure 4.11 or display on an overhead projector. Optional information is set off by brackets, and ellipses indicate where students need to complete paragraphs with their own sentences.

The *U.S. News & World Report* Best Colleges report ranks colleges by seven factors, one of which is student selectivity. The Web site http://www.usnews.com/articles/education/best-colleges/2008/08/21/how-we-calculate-the-rankings.html?PageNr=3 (accessed December 24, 2009) states

> Student selectivity (15 percent). A school's academic atmosphere is determined in part by the abilities and ambitions of the student body. We factor in the admissions test scores of all enrollees who took the Critical Reading and Math portions of the SAT and the Composite ACT score (50 percent of the selectivity score); the proportion of enrolled freshmen (for all national universities and liberal arts colleges) who graduated in the top 10 percent of their high school classes . . . (40 percent); and the acceptance rate, or the ratio of students admitted to applicants (10 percent).

Today's date

[Recipient Name]

[Title]

[School Name]

[Street Address] [or e-mail address, instead of street address information]

[City, ST ZIP Code]

Dear Admissions Counselor [Recipient Name]:

First paragraph: I am interested in applying for undergraduate admission to [College Name] because of my interest in. . . .

Second paragraph: My current academic accomplishments are. . . .

Third paragraph: I have special (playing, teaching, leadership) skills in. . . .

Fourth paragraph: By the time I am a high school senior, I anticipate. . . .

Fifth paragraph: I believe I would be a productive part of [College Name] because. . . .

Signature area:

[Please send me application materials, a catalog, an academic calendar, and a schedule of courses.]

Sincerely,

Your Name

[Street Address] [or e-mail address, instead of street address information]

[City, ST ZIP Code]

Figure 4.11.
Letter template.

University chess programs want to attract top students who are also top chess players. Appendix C has a list of colleges and universities with chess on campus. Appendix C also highlights colleges and universities that give chess scholarships. YouTube has videos from different university chess programs. Here are two choices from UTD: http://www.youtube.com/watch?v=_hW75TD0x48 and http://www.youtube.com/watch?v=ZsZsT3Q-Pnw. If these URLs change, type in the search terms "UTD chess program" into the YouTube search box.

Optional: Students may mail or e-mail their letters to universities. If this option is chosen, make available resources such as college guides or the Internet (for researching higher education Web sites) available. Then each student can find the mailing address (or e-mail address) and name of an admissions counselor at his or her desired university. If students mail or e-mail their letters, colleges and universities will respond with information.

Procedure

Ask students what colleges look for when deciding on scholarships for students. List their responses on the dry-erase board. Then ask students why a college wants good students. After writing their responses on the dry-erase board, share that colleges are ranked, in part, by the quality of their student bodies. To support the ranking of a university, a university's chess program needs to attract good students. To field a winning team, the chess program also needs to attract top chess players. Show a YouTube or other promotional video for a university chess program. I showed http://www.youtube.com/watch?v=_hW75TD0x48, a five-minute segment about the UTD Chess Program.

After watching the video segment, students write first-person letters to college admissions officers. Give the following directions while displaying Figure 4.11 (or distributing copies of Figure 4.11 to students). The five-paragraph letter should have a first paragraph stating the student's interest in the university. The second paragraph should highlight the student's current academic accomplishments. The third paragraph should describe the student's chess or other special skills (such as music, art, or athletics), including playing or teaching skills. In the fourth paragraph, students should predict their academic and chess (or other special area) level by the time they are high school seniors. In the fifth paragraph, students should express their desire to be a productive part of the university and the university chess program (or other special area).

Optional: Each student researches which university to send his or her letter to and sends it to that university's admissions counselor. If this option is chosen, include an enhanced signature section. Instead of just a signature, the section should include a request for information to be sent to the student at his or her home address or home e-mail as shown in Figure 4.11. Build in extra time for students to find admissions counselor contact information. The name of the admissions counselor and the university's address should be at the top of the page, as shown in Figure 4.11. In many cases, students may be able to save postage by e-mailing their requests for information to e-mail addresses or Web sites provided by universities.

Evaluation

Evaluate the letters on how well the students followed your directions for each paragraph. Letters written by SMS chess advisory students are in Appendix A.

White to move and mate in nine

From Alvarez versus Ballom, round 3

Figure 4.12.
Pan Am Chess Position.

Figure 4.13.
Stephanie Ballom.

Exercise 14: Check 'em Tech

Teacher Background

The Pan American Intercollegiate Team Chess Championship (Pan Am) is open to teams from colleges and universities in North and South America. Traditionally held between Christmas and New Year's Day, when students are between semesters, the 2008 event was December 27–30 in Fort Worth, Texas. Twenty-nine teams competed.

Each Pan Am team has four players, plus a maximum of two alternates. A four-board match can be tied 2–2. Match points matter the most in this six-round tournament. In 2008, UTD and the University of Maryland, Baltimore County tied for first place by winning four matches and tying two matches.

In the third round, Figure 4.12 occurred in the game of National Master Ernesto Alvarez (Miami Dade College) versus Stephanie Ballom, Texas Tech University (TTU). TTU won this match 2.5–1.5. Figure 4.13 is a photo of Stephanie Ballom at the Pan Am.

Procedure and Materials

Set up Figure 4.12 on the demonstration board. Or write this notation on the dry-erase board, White: Kc1; Qe3; R's d1, g1; Bc2, Nf6; P's a3, d4, e5, f2. Black: Kg7; Qa5; R's a8, f8; Bc8; Nb8; P's a7, b7, c3, f7, g6, h7. White to move and checkmate in nine.

Inform students of the procedure for solving the problem. After setting up the position on the board, each person in the pair will write a proposed solution in notation. Then each person will take turns showing his or her proposed solution by moving the chessmen on the board. After each person has presented, the pair moves the chessmen and debates which ideas look promising.

Pass out sets and boards to pairs of students. Students also need pencils and paper for writing algebraic notation. If pairs request help, share the first move from the solution in Appendix A. Consider allowing students to work more at home or during the next class period. Have students turn in their algebraically notated answers.

Expected Time

20 minutes. 5 minutes for supplies. 10 minutes for pairs or groups to work on the problem. 5 minutes to show the continuation played from Figure 4.12.

Evaluation

Show what actually happened after Figure 4.12. Alvarez chose an incorrect move, 23. Rdf1. Stephanie Ballom's continuation fit her team's slogan of Check 'em Tech, with Stephanie giving check in 6 of the last 11 moves **23. Rdf1 Qxa3+ 24. Kd1 Qa1+ 25. Ke2 Qa6+ 26. Kf3 Rh8 27. Rh1 h5 28. Qg5 Nc6 29. Nxh5+ Kf8 30. Nf6 Nxd4+ 31. Kg2 Bh3+!** (TTU Coach GM Susan Polgar said that 31....Bh3+ was "definitely an exclamation point move") **32. Rxh3 Rxh3 33. Kxh3 Qxf1+ 0–1.** White's best continuation—the solution for Figure 4.12—is in Appendix A. Correct the students' answers using Appendix A.

Lesson 15: Immigration

Objectives

Students match reasons to policies. Students recommend maintaining or changing the USCF's one-year residency requirement for representing the United States in the **Olympiad.**

NCSS Theme

X. Civic Ideals & Practices.

Materials and Sources

Photocopy Figure 4.14, one copy per student.

For background I read Benjamin (2007). Benjamin wrote about growing up as an American-born chess prodigy and about his years as a Grandmaster. Benjamin favored "developing homegrown talent versus importing developed products" (p. 247). Benjamin wrote (p. 248):

> When Russian chessplayers first began to arrive on our shores they provided competition necessary to stimulate American talent. But the numbers have gotten so out of whack that any young player would be discouraged from a career as a professional player.

Procedure

Tell about the Olympiad and the U.S. teams that compete in it. The Olympiad is organized by FIDE every two years. In 2008, 100 coun-

Name_____

Match the policies on the top half of the page with the reasons on the bottom half. Two reasons support each policy. Write the numbers of the two reasons in the blanks beside the letter of the policy. Background information: The USCF (United States Chess Federation) selects two Olympiad teams, a men's team and a women's team.

Policies:

_____ _____ A. Require three years of residency in the United States to play on the Olympiad teams.

_____ _____ B. Require one year of residency in the United States to play on the Olympiad teams.

_____ _____ C. Require U.S. citizenship to play on the Olympiad teams.

Reasons:

1. Since several other countries require citizenship to play for their Olympiad teams, the USCF would have an unfair competitive advantage if it allowed highly rated, noncitizen chess players on its Olympiad teams.

2. The USCF wants the very best players on its Olympiad teams as soon as possible.

3. Players should compete on a U.S. Olympiad team only after they have established a U.S. fan base, which takes two or three years of magazine articles and newspaper reports about the player.

4. It is unfair to homegrown players if the Olympiad spots that they have worked hard to earn are taken by citizens of other countries.

5. If an immigrant plays well enough to be on an Olympiad team, he or she should get to play on that team right away.

6. To function as a team, players should all speak English well, prove their loyalty to the United States, and train together over two or three years.

Figure 4.14.
Reasons for USCF policy on immigrants.

tries sent men's and women's teams. United States players covet the all-expense paid trip to compete with the world's best. The USCF wants to send players who will perform well internationally and who have an established fan base in the United States. Yet many of the best players in the United States have recently moved here. Tell students that they will match reasons to policies on Figure 4.14. Then they will vote on what the USCF policy should be about allowing immigrants to play on the Olympiad team. At the end of class, they will learn what the USCF policy is.

Pass out copies of Figure 4.14 for students to complete individually. After everyone has completed Figure 4.14, take a straw poll on whether the USCF policy should be one year of residency, three years of residency, or citizenship to be a part of an Olympiad team. After the initial poll, ask if anyone wants to present more reasons before the official vote. After students present, vote again.

Then tell students what the policies of USCF have been. Before 2003, the USCF required three years of residency to play on an Olympiad team. In 2003, the USCF changed the requirement to one year. The USCF has never required citizenship to play on an Olympiad team.

Evaluation

You may grade students' answers for Figure 4.14 using the answer key in Appendix A.

Exercise 15: Foreign Chess Terms

Teacher Background

One might speak of feeling like a pawn at work, or write about a politician being checkmated by his rival. Such assimilated chess terms derive from many languages. Checkmate, for example, comes from the Persian term *shāh māt,* meaning the king is exhausted (Yalom, 2004, p. 5). Several chess terms are part of standard American discourse.

In this exercise, students learn some foreign chess terms that are not part of our normal discourse. Each term, however, describes an important chess concept. Definitions for the terms, in this exercise and in Figure 4.15, are in the glossary. Or check Appendix A for the answer key to Figure 4.15. For the seven terms in this exercise, the j'adoube pronunciation is from Eade (2005, p. 327) and the other pronunciations are from Bill Wall (in the comments section for the posting http://blog.chess.com/SonofPearl/zwischenzug-bless-you).

Procedure and Materials

Make photocopies of Figure 4.15 (one per student) to pass out at the end of the procedure. One chess set and board for every group of students (seven groups are needed for the procedure).

Match the foreign chess terms (1–7) with their meanings (a–g). The terms are listed alphabetically on the top half of this worksheet. The meanings are listed below all the terms. Put the letter of the correct definition next to the number of the term that it defines.

_____1. en passant

_____2. en prise

_____3. fianchetto

_____4. j'adoube

_____5. luft

_____6. zugzwang

_____7. zwischenzug

a. Italian meaning "little flank." Refers to developing a bishop along the long diagonal.

b. German for a situation in which to move is to lose.

c. French for "I adjust."

d. French for "in passing." Refers to a special pawn capture.

e. German for an in-between move.

f. German for air. Refers to a situation in which one moves a pawn to create an escape square for one's king.

g. French for "in take." Refers to putting a chessman where it may be taken for free, or leaving a chessman in such a dangerous situation.

Figure 4.15.
Foreign terms in chess.

Remind students that many terms from chess, such as checkmate, originally came from other languages but are now part of English. Checkmate came from the Persian *shāh māt,* meaning the king is exhausted.

Tell students that chess contains a number of foreign words common to chess, but which are not yet used in everyday English conversation. Put the seven terms from Figure 4.15 on the dry-erase board. Those terms (with pronunciation in parentheses) are: en passant (ahn pah-SAHNT), en prise (ahn PREEZ), **fianchetto** (fee-an-KET-toe), **j'adoube** (juh-DOOB), **luft, zugzwang** (TSOOKS-vahng), and **zwischenzug** (TSV-EYE-shun-tsook). As you say and point to each word, have the students repeat after you.

Explain that each group will be assigned one term. For that term, the group will construct a chess position that demonstrates the term. Calculate how many students need to be in each group. There needs to be seven groups, one group for each term. Then assign the terms and give each group a board and set. If a group asks for help, because it does not know its assigned term, set up the appropriate one of Figures 4.16–4.21 on its board as an example. You may also read the glossary definition of the

Black has just played 14....g5

Gaudersen-Faul, 1928. 15. hxg6 e.p.#

Figure 4.16.
En passant.

White had played 31. Rc8+ Kh7

Holdeman-W. Root, 2008; 32. Rc7? Nxe4!

Figure 4.17.
A knight left en prise.

Black's Bb7 and Bg7 are fianchettoed

White's Bb2 and Bg2 are fianchettoed

Figure 4.18.
Fianchettoed bishops.

White to move and create luft

Root-Altschuler, 2007; I played h4

Figure 4.19.
Moving pawn for luft.

The person on move will lose a pawn

Example of zugzwang

Figure 4.20.
Zugzwang.

Black has just erred with 17....Nd5xe3?

Clarissa Root-J. King. 2006; 18. Nxe7+

Figure 4.21.
Zwischenzug.

term to the group. After the group sees the example and hears the defini-tion, group members should construct their own example position.

Here are the example positions for each term. Figure 4.16 illustrates en passant and is from Chernev (1955, p. 136). In Figure 4.17, white checked the black king on the previous move (move 31) but then forgot that his N on e4 is hanging. He played **32. Rc7?,** which left the knight en prise. William responded with **32....Nxe4!** Figure 4.18 shows fianchet-tos. In Figure 4.19, I would like to play dxc6 and be a queen ahead. But if I played that, black would respond Rxd1#. Therefore, I created luft so that the capture on d1 would not allow a back-rank mate. Figure 4.20 is from Pandolfini (1995, p. 248). He called this particular endgame, zugz-wang, a trebuchet (tre-byu-SHET or trey-byu-SHAY), but I had not heard that term before. In Figure 4.21, the recapture on e3 leads to an equal po-sition after 18. fxe3 Rxd2 19. Nxe7+. Better is 18. Rxd8+ Bxd8 19. fxe3. But best is what Clarissa played, the zwischenzug of **18. Nxe7+!** Later she can recapture on e3 with a huge advantage. There is no position for j'adoube because, from any position, saying j'adoube means "I adjust," and the group can wiggle a piece or pawn to demonstrate.

Once you have determined that each group's position represents its assigned term, allow members of each group to visit other groups. That is, half of each group's members stay home with their term and position to explain it to visitors. The other half of each group's members travels to the other groups to learn the six other terms. Then the two halves switch roles. When I taught this plan, I told students that they would be voting on which group explained its term best and was most polite to visitors.

Pass out Figure 4.15 and have students complete it individually.

Expected Time

25 minutes. 20 minutes for group work. 5 minutes for students to com-plete Figure 4.15.

Evaluation

Grade Figure 4.15 using the answer key in Appendix A. Based on your own evaluation of each group's position, and the students voting, you can determine which group was most effective at conveying their knowledge of their assigned term.

Chapter 5

CHESS BASICS

Rules of Chess

Starting position of a chess game

Queen on her own color

Figure 5.1.
Starting position.

Let's Play Chess

Chess is a game for two players, one with the white chessmen and one with the black chessmen. Pieces refer to the kings, queens, rooks, bishops, and knights only. Pawns are called pawns. At the beginning of the game, the chessmen are set up as shown in Figure 5.1. These hints will help you remember the proper board setup:

1. Opposing kings and queens go directly opposite each other.
2. The square in each player's lower right hand corner is a light (white) one. Remember the expression "light on right."
3. The white queen goes on a light square, and the black queen on a dark square.

The Chessmen and How They Move

White always moves first, and then the players take turns moving. Only one piece or pawn may be moved at each turn (except for castling, as explained later in this chapter under the heading "Special Moves"). Chessmen move along unblocked lines. But the knight also may jump over other chessmen. You may not move a chessman to a square already occupied by your own pawn or piece. But you may capture an

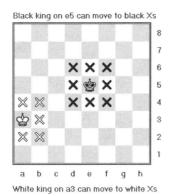

Black king on e5 can move to black Xs

White king on a3 can move to white Xs

Figure 5.2.
Moves of the king (K).

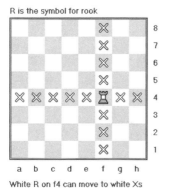

Black queen is on the square c6

Legal moves are marked with black Xs

Figure 5.3.
Moves of the queen (Q).

R is the symbol for rook

White R on f4 can move to white Xs

Figure 5.4.
Moves of the rook (R).

opponent's chessman that stands on a square where one of your chessmen can move. Simply remove the opponent's piece or pawn from the board and put your own chessman in its place (except for the en passant pawn capture, as explained in "Special Moves"). Although touching pieces and pawns may be helpful when solving chess problems, the touch move rule should apply in every chess game where wins, losses, and draws are recorded.

Generally speaking, the side with the stronger army will win. The strength of your army is determined by its point value. For example, trading a knight (worth three points) for a queen (worth nine points) is usually a good idea, because the **trade** leaves you the equivalent of six points ahead. The value of a pawn is one point, so a knight is worth three pawns or three points.

The King

The king has the symbol K. The graphic ♔ represents the white king, and ♚ is the black king. When the king is checkmated his whole army loses. Therefore, in one sense, the king's point value is infinite. However, his actual value as an attacker is generally about three points, according to Wolff (2005, p. 76) and close to four points in the endgame, according to USCF and Kurzdorfer (2003, p. 96). The king can move one square in any direction—for example, to any of the squares with Xs in Figure 5.2. The king may never move into check—that is, onto a square attacked by an opponent's piece or pawn. If conditions are correct, the king may castle once per game (explained in "Special Moves").

The Queen

The queen is the most powerful piece and has the symbol Q. The graphic ♕ represents the white queen, and ♛ is the black queen. The queen is worth nine points. If her path is not blocked, the queen can move any number of squares horizontally, vertically, or diagonally. She can reach any of the squares with black Xs in Figure 5.3.

The Rook

The rook is the next most powerful piece and has the symbol R. The graphic ♖ represents the white rooks, and ♜ symbolizes the black rooks. The rook is worth five points. The rook can move any number of squares vertically or horizontally if its path is not blocked. The rook can reach any of the squares with white Xs in Figure 5.4.

The Bishop

The bishop has the symbol B and has the graphic ♗ for white's bishops and ♝ for black's bishops. The bishop is generally

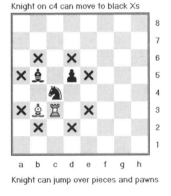

Figure 5.5.
Moves of the bishop (B).

considered to be worth three points, though some chess writers place the bishop's value slightly higher. For example, Wolff (2005, p. 75) wrote, "3 points (plus a teensy bit more)." The bishop can move any number of squares diagonally if its path is not blocked. At the beginning of the game, each side has one light-squared bishop and one dark-squared bishop. In Figure 5.5, the white bishop on c1 is white's dark- or black-squared bishop. It must stay on the black squares, marked by white Xs. In Figure 5.5, black's bishop on c8 is a light or white-squared bishop. It can move to the white squares marked by black Xs.

The Knight

The knight has the symbol N and has the graphic ♘ for white's knights and ♞ for black's knights. The knight is worth three points. The knight may hop over any chessmen in between its old and new squares. Think of the knight's move as the capital letter "L." It moves two squares horizontally, or two squares vertically, and then makes a right-angle turn onto its destination square. The knight always lands on a square opposite in color from its prior square. Figure 5.6 shows the N's moves with black Xs.

The Pawn

Figure 5.6.
Moves of the knight (N).

The pawn has the symbol P, but pawn moves are notated by stating the square the pawn moves to without use of the P. The graphic symbol for the white pawns is ♙, and the symbol for the black pawns is ♟. A pawn is worth one point (one pawn). The pawn moves straight ahead (never backward), but it captures diagonally. It moves one square at a time, but on its first move it has the option of moving forward one or two squares.

In Figure 5.7, the circles indicate possible destinations for the pawns. The white pawn is on its original square, so it may move ahead either one or two squares. The black pawn has previously moved, so it may move ahead only one square at a time. The squares on which these pawns may make captures are indicated by Xs. However, captures would only be possible if enemy chessmen were on the X-ed squares.

If a pawn advances to the opposite end of the board, it is immediately promoted to a piece. It may not remain a pawn or become a king. One can promote a pawn to a queen (or R, or N, or B) even if one still has the original piece(s) on the board. In Figure 5.7, the promotion square for the white pawn is e8 and the promotion square for the black pawn is b1.

Special Moves

There are two special moves in the game of chess. The first, castling, occurs in almost every chess game between experienced

Figure 5.7.
Moves of the pawn (P).

chess players. The second, en passant, is possible in less than 1 game out of 10 (USCF & Kurzdorfer, 2003, p. 62).

Figure 5.8.
Before castling.

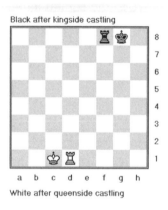

Figure 5.9.
After castling.

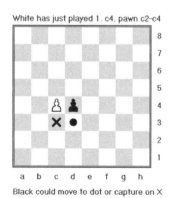

Figure 5.10.
The en passant (e.p.) rule.

Castling

Each player may castle only once during a game, when certain conditions are met. Castling lets a player move two pieces at once: the king and one rook. Castling allows you to place your king in a safe location and also allows the castled rook to become more active. When the move is legal, each player has the choice of castling kingside or queenside or not at all, no matter what the other player chooses to do.

The procedure for castling is to move your king two squares toward the king's rook (kingside) or two squares toward the queen's rook (queenside). At the same time, the rook involved goes to the square beside the king and toward the center of the board. Kingside castling is sometimes called "castling short" and queenside castling is "castling long" (Khmelnitsky, Khodarkovsky, & Zadorozny, 2006, Book 1, p. 89; King, 2000, p. 26). Figures 5.8 and 5.9 show castling.

In order to castle, neither the king nor the rook involved may have moved before. Also, the king may not castle out of check, into check, or through check. Furthermore, there may not be pieces of either color between the king and the rook involved in castling.

En Passant (e.p.)

This French phrase, meaning "in passing," is used to describe a special pawn capture. When one player moves a pawn two squares forward so that it is on an adjacent file and the same rank as an opponent's pawn, that opponent's pawn can capture the double-jumping pawn as if it had only moved one square. However, if the opponent's pawn does not exercise the en passant capture immediately, the option disappears for that particular e.p. capture. But new opportunities may arise for pawns in similar circumstances.

The rule originated when pawns gained the double-jump power on their first move, which occurred shortly after the 1450s (King, 2000, pp. 8, 27). To keep some consistency despite the rule change, the en passant rule arose so that one could capture the double-jumping pawn as if it had only moved one square. Figure 5.10 shows black's choices. If black takes en passant (1....dxc3 e.p.), his black pawn ends up on c3 and white's pawn on c4 is removed from the board.

About Check, Checkmate, and Stalemate

The ultimate goal of chess is to checkmate your opponent's king. The king is not actually captured and removed from the board. But if the king is attacked (checked), it must get out of check immediately. If there is no way to get out of check, then the position is a checkmate. The side that is checkmated loses.

You may not move into check. For example, moving into a direct line with your opponent's rook if there are no chessmen between the rook and your king is an **illegal** move. The rook could "capture" your king, which is not allowed.

If you are put into check by your opponent's move, there are three ways of getting out of check:

1. Capture the attacker.
2. Place one of your own chessmen between the attacker and your king. Blockading doesn't work if the attacker is a knight or a pawn.
3. Move your king away from the attack.

If a checked player has none of these three escapes, then he is checkmated and loses the game. In a chess tournament, a checkmate is scored as a win (one point) for the player delivering the checkmate.

In contrast, if a player is not in check but has no legal move, the position is called a stalemate. A stalemate is scored as a draw or tie (half a point) for each player.

These rules of chess were adapted from *Let's Play Chess,* a brochure formerly available from the United States Chess Federation. The next two sections of chapter 5—"Win, Lose, or Draw" and "Reading and Writing Chess"—illustrate what happens when chess games are underway.

Win, Lose, or Draw

As noted in the rules of chess, checkmate or stalemate ends a chess game. A check, however, is temporary. When the king escapes from check, the game continues. Figure 5.11 has exercises to identify check, checkmate, and stalemate. The answer key for Figure 5.11 is in Appendix A. Stalemate is just one of several ways that chess games can be drawn; see *draws* in the Glossary.

In addition to losing by being checkmated, you can also lose a game by resigning (giving up). Beginners should usually continue playing until checkmate rather than resigning. Although wins keep your spirits up, losses educate by showing where your moves went wrong. In the hotel elevator at a major scholastic tournament, I met a little girl in a chess shirt and her mom. I asked the girl how her previous game went. She said, "I learned." Her mom clarified, "That's what we say when she loses, because we learn when we lose."

Reading and Writing Chess

Playing chess games is one way to improve at chess; learning chess notation is another improvement method. Reading notation enables you to study games published in chess columns in newspapers, in chess

Name _____

For each diagram, tell whether the position is a check, a mate (checkmate), or a stalemate. Write

your answer in the space below the diagram.

Black to move. Check, mate, or stalemate

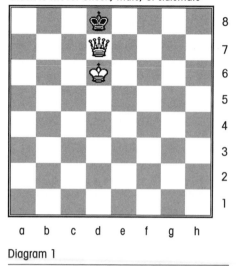

Diagram 1

Black to move. Check, mate, or stalemate

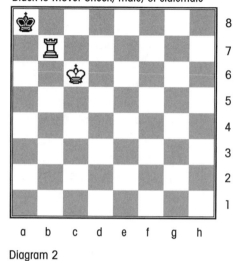

Diagram 2

White to move. Check, mate, or stalemate

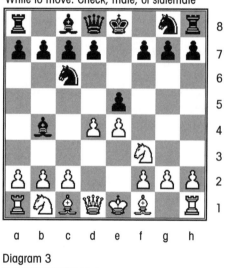

Diagram 3

White to move. Check, mate, or stalemate

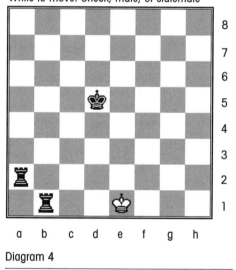

Diagram 4

Figure 5.11.
Check, checkmate, or stalemate?

magazines, and in chess books. Notating your own chess games allows you to review those games later with a friend, parent, teacher, or chess coach.

To practice algebraic chess notation, I present the first six moves of the Exchange Variation of the French **Defense**. The French is characterized by black's first move of 1....e6. The defense is named after an 1834 correspondence match between the cities of London and Paris. There are many examples of the French Defense available, in chess books and on the Internet. The moves below are taken from the game José Raúl Capablanca–Géza Maróczy, Lake Hopatcong, New Jersey,1926. This game is available on many Internet sites, for example, http://www.chessgames. com/perl/chessgame?gid=1094365.

1. e4 e6 2. d4 d5 3. exd5 exd5 4.Bd3 Bd6 5.Nf3 Nf6 6.0-0 0-0

Now I will explain how each move was notated. **1. e4.** Figure 5.12 shows the move 1. e4 on the board. The white pawn that sits in front of the white king moved two squares forward. The square is named e4,

Figure 5.12.

Figure 5.13.

Figure 5.14.

Figure 5.15.

Figure 5.16.

Figure 5.17.

derived from the file-name (e) and the rank name (4). When a pawn (P) moves there, we could write Pe4, but it is traditional not to list the P when notating pawn moves. **1....e6.** The ellipses (...) before the move lets us know that the pawn move e6 was a move for black. Figure 5.13 shows the position after black moved the pawn in front of his king one square forward. **2. d4.** The position after white's second move is shown in Figure 5.14. **2....d5.** Black replied with a pawn's move from d7 to d5. The resulting position is shown in Figure 5.15. **3. exd5.** The "x" means capture. The "e" represents the file that the capturing pawn was on before it captured. The resulting position is shown in Figure 5.16. Now follow the next couple of moves in your head or on a board. **3....exd5 4. Bd3.** The B means the bishop moved to d3. **4....Bd6 5. Nf3.** The N means a knight has moved. N is for knight, K is for king. **5....Nf6 6. 0–0.** This notation means kingside castling. You can use zeroes or capital letter O's for castling. Queenside castling is written 0-0-0. Other special symbols are +, written at the end of a move to show that the move gave a check; # or + + designates giving checkmate. **6....0-0.** Black's sixth move is also castling. The position after black's sixth move is shown in Figure 5.17. Does the position in Figure 5.17 match what you visualized or played out on your board? If so, good job!

Appendix A

ANSWER KEY

Chapter 2

Lesson 1 refers to an eighth grader's timeline and historical-continuity paragraph. Figure A.1 is his timeline. Figure A.2 is his paragraph.

Exercise 1 (Figure 2.1). Answer key is Figure A.3.

Lesson 2 (Figure 2.2). Answer key is Figure A.4.

Exercise 2. **1. Nh5+ Rxh5 2. Rxg6+ Kxg6 3. Re6# 1–0.**

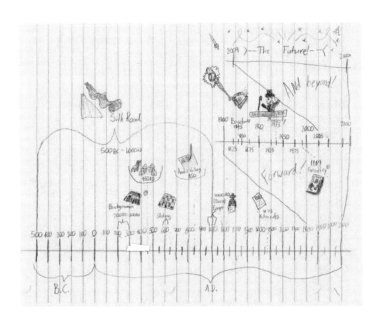

Figure A.1.
A student's timeline.

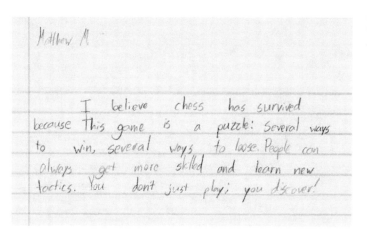

Matthew M.

I believe chess has survived because this game is a puzzle: several ways to win, several ways to loose. People can always get more skilled and learn new tactics. You dont just play; you discover!

Figure A.2.
A student's paragraph.

Answers for Figure 2.1 are in column 6 below.

1	2	3	4	5	6
Persia, chatrang (600)	*Arabic, shatranj (850)*	*Meaning*	*Rules of movement from shatranj*	*Modern rules for chess, Europe, 1475. Exception: Castling only became standard after 1600.*	*Name today*
Shah	Shah	King	One square in any direction. May not stay in, or move into, check. No castling.	Same as column 4, except that kings can castle once per game.	**King**
Farzin	Firz or Firzan	Counselor or Vizier	Moves only one diagonal square at a time.	May choose, for each turn, to move either like a rook or like a bishop.	**Queen**
Pil	Fil	Elephant	Jumps to second diagonal square. Never occupies first diagonal square.	Moves on unobstructed squares on a diagonal.	**Bishop**
Asp	Faras	Horse	Moves in a capital L: 2 squares horizontally then 1 square vertically, or 2 squares vertically and then 1 horizontally.	Same as column 4.	**Knight**
Rukh	Rukh	Chariot	Moves on unobstructed files and ranks.	Column 4, plus castling.	**Rook**
Pujada	Baidaq	Foot Soldier	Moves forward one unob-structed square. Promotes to Firzan on back rank.	Column 4, plus optional two-square jump on 1st move. Promotes to Q, R, B, or N.	**Pawn**

Figure A.3.
Answer key for Figure 2.1.

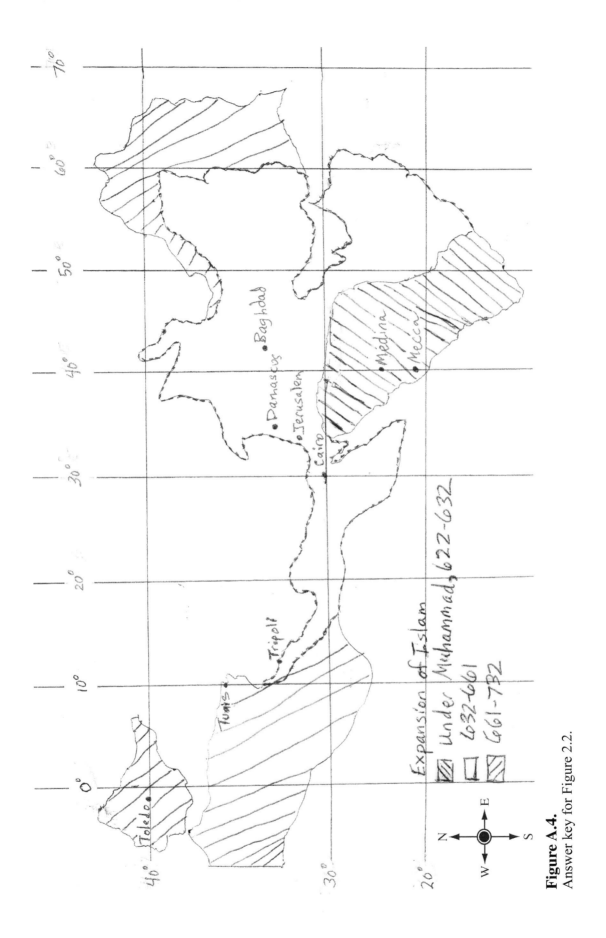

Figure A.4.
Answer key for Figure 2.2.

From *People, Places, Checkmates: Teaching Social Studies with Chess* by Alexey W. Root. Santa Barbara, CA: Libraries Unlimited. Copyright © 2010.

Figure A.5.
Silk Road paragraph.

Names Ryan Eric Coleman

Death of a Son

      In ancient India, a queen's son died from battle fatigue. The queen's council wanted to show the queen what had happened. The council asked a wise man for help. With the assistance of a carpenter, the wise man created chess. The wise man and the carpenter played a chess game for the queen. At the end of the game, one king was in shāh māt, a Persian term that means the king is exhausted. Thus, the queen learned that her son died of battle fatigue rather than at the hands of another soldier. The purposes of chess in *Death of a Son*: war isn't heroic and you can die from exaution.

Doubling of the Squares

      A wise man invented chess, and presented it to an Indian king. The king was delighted with the game, and asked its inventor to name a reward. The wise man asked for one grain of wheat on the first square of the chessboard, two on the second, four on the third, and that the doubling of grains continue in this pattern until the sixty-fourth square. When the king realized that eighteen quintillion grains would be needed, he learned an important lesson. The purposes of chess in *Doubling of the Squares*: Be careful what you promise. Don't underestimate a wise man. (Math)

Prince and Princess

      A Muslim prince plays chess against a Christian princess. During the game, he is distracted by her beautiful face and loses. They fall in love, and the Christian princess is converted to Islam. The purposes of chess in *Prince and Princess*: Love

Figure A.6.
Group's answers for Figure 2.11.

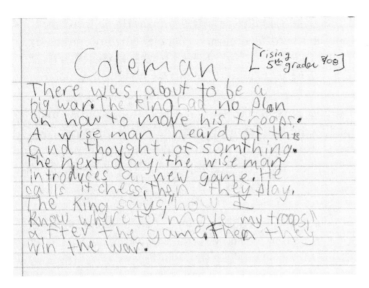

Figure A.7.
A fifth-grade student's legend.

Lesson 3 refers to a seventh grader's paragraph about the Silk Road, which is Figure A.5. He was student #16 in the role play.

Exercise 3. Tandem chess has no answer key.

Lesson 4 (Figure 2.11). Answer key is Figure A.6, from a group composed of a rising fourth grader, a rising fifth grader, and a rising seventh grader.

Exercise 4. **1. Rh8+ Kxh8 2. Be5+ Kg8 3. Rh8+ Kxh8 4. f7# 1–0.**

Lesson 5. Figure A.7, an example of such a short legend, was written by a rising fifth grader.

Following are three of my SMS chess advisory students' legends with accompanying chess problems. William, seventh grade, read Charlemagne's pilgrimage to Jerusalem (Guerber, 1986).

Charles the Great (white king) went on a pilgrimage to Jerusalem. He took three of his paladins (white pawns). When they arrived in Jerusalem, each paladin made a boast. The King of Jerusalem (black king) bade them to fulfill their boasts. One paladin succeeded and married a princess. White: Ka1; P's e4, e5, h3. Black: Ke6. White to move. **1. h4 Kxe5 2. h5 Kf6 3. Kb2 Kg5 4. Kc3 Kxh5 5. Kd4 Kg6 6. Ke5** and white wins this king and pawn ending. The paladin's promotion is like marrying a princess because a white queen appears for him to marry.

Winning the ending will follow the same procedure as in chapter 2's exercise 5-B.

Jared, seventh grade, read two legends during our class visit to the library. The first was about King Arthur. The second was about Pecos Bill, in Leach (1958). Figure A.8 is his Pecos Bill notes. Jared wrote the following legend:

Pecos Bill (the pawn) was raised by wolves and as a wolf. He thought he was a wolf for his childhood. One day, some men (the king and

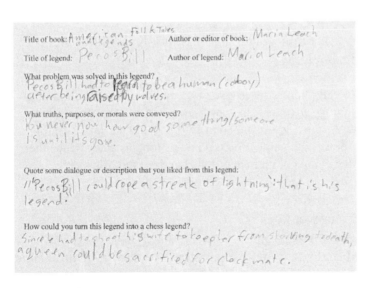

Figure A.8.
A student's notes while reading a legend.

the bishop) came along and told him he was a human. He believed them, and he worked long and hard to become a famous cowboy (promote). White: Kf3; Bf7; Pg6. Black: Ke7; Ng7. **1. Kg4 Kf8 2. Kg5 Ne8 3. Bxe8 Kxe8 4. Kh6 Kf8 5. Kh7 Ke7 6. g7 Kf7 7. g8(Q)+ resigns 1–0.**

Kyler, seventh grade, missed the first and second sessions (instruction and library) because he had been in study hall. When he returned to chess advisory, he saw other students polishing their legends and creating chess problems. He wanted to write one too and asked if he could base his on Greek mythology.

The Minotaur is the black queen. The Minotaur got angry and tried to get out of the maze at the same time as Theseus (the white king) and his lover Ariadne, who is King Minos's daughter (the white pawn), went to slay the Minotaur. Theseus and Ariadne used a ball of magical yarn (the white knight) to escape. White: Kh6; Ne3; P's a6, b6, c4, c7, d5, g6. Black: Kh8; Qb7. Black to move. **1....Qxa6 2. Ng4 Qxc4 3. Nf6 Qxd5 4. g7# 1–0.**

Exercise 5-A. The checkmate designed by Luis, eighth grade, reminded me of that of Al-Adli in chapter 2's exercise 2. In both solutions, the king's own chessmen blocked escape squares and the mate was delivered by a rook.

Chess problem to accompany *Death of a Son*. White: Kd3; Rf2; Bh4; Ng5; P's b4, e2, f4. Black: Kg7; R's c8, e8; P's b5, f5. Black to move. **1.... Red8+ 2. Ke3 Rc3# 0–1.** The chess problem shows the queen which rook ended her son's life.

Exercise 5-B's answer is within the exercise.

Chapter 3

Lesson 6 refers to a seventh grader's paragraph. Kyler titled his paragraph Chess and Technology.

Before the time of cell phones, messaging was much, much, much, much slower. So as technology advances, so does the way we talk to people. Chess is also an example. As the rules [changed in 1475], so did the speed. Before the queen got her power the games could go on as long as a day. Once the queen got power the game got more aggressive, angry, and less merry.

Exercise 6 has no answer key.
Lesson 7 has no answer key.
Exercise 7 has no answer key.
Lesson 8 asked students to write a paragraph or draw a picture. Here is a "Recall of Columbus" paragraph by William, seventh grade:

Columbus rode on a white horse, as he moved on the road. Suddenly, he paused, "Who is the rider dressed in black behind me?" The rider rode up and said, "I have come from their majesties bidding you to return." "And I shall go to them," said Columbus.

Here is another "Recall of Columbus" paragraph, by Noah, eighth grade:

After having his plan to explore uncharted waters for a trade route to the Indies rejected by King Ferdinand and Queen Isabella of Spain, Columbus started on his way to make his proposition to the French. Only six miles away from where he left he received a message from the King saying that Spain would fund his voyage. So he decided to turn around and take Spain up on its offer.

Figure A.9.
A student's "Recall of Columbus" drawing.

Figure A.9 is a drawing by Jared, seventh grade.

Exercise 8. **1. Rg8+ Rxg8 2. Rf8+ Rxf8 3. e7+ Qe6 4. Bxe6# 1–0.**

Lesson 9 has no answer key.

Exercise 9. The side that moves second gets into zugzwang. Moving loses a pawn, and with it the game. One possible line is **1. c5 Kb5 2. Kh2 f4 3. Kg2 g4 4. Kg1 h3 5. Kh2 f3 6. Kg3 Ka6** (or 6....f2 7. Kxf2 h2 8. Kg2 g3 9. Kh1 Kxb4 10. c6 and the white pawn will promote) **7. c6 Ka7 8. b5 Kb8 9. b6 Kc8 10. a6 f2 11. a7 Kd8 12. a8(Q)+ 1–0.**

Lesson 10. The answer key for Figure 3.7 is Figure A.10. The answer key for Figure 3.8 is Figure A.11. Both Figures A.10 and A.11 are from the first term, 10th month (October), of the Obama presidency.

Exercise 10. **1. e5 Rb6 2. e6 Rb1 3. Kf6.** If instead white played 3. Rh4, intending to block black's perpetual check, then the following would occur: 3....Rf1+ 4. Ke5 Re1+ 5. Re4 Rxe4+ 6. Kxe4 Ke7 7. Ke5 Ke8 8. Kd6. In contrast to the king and pawn versus king endgame in exercise 5-B, white's king is not in front of his pawn. Therefore, white cannot use the opposition to drive black away from the promotion square (e8). 8....Kd8 9. e7+ Ke8 10. Ke6. This position is a draw by stalemate. Black is not in check, yet has no legal moves. **3....Rf1+ 4. Ke5 Re1+ 5. Kd5 Rd1+ 6. Ke4 Re1+.** If the white king does not choose 7. Kd5 or 7. Kf5 to defend his e-pawn, black will play 7....Rxe6 with a draw. **7. Kf5 Rf1+ 8. Ke5 Re1+.** Black has perpetual check, so the game is drawn, 1/2–1/2.

Chapter 4

Lesson 11. For Figure 4.1, part I, students should have put Xs by 1, 3, 4, 5, 7, 8, and 9.

Here are three eighth graders' answers for Part II. Noah wrote:

This is one possible answer key for Figure 3.7, with political leaders as of October, 2009.

Symbol	Title	Name of Current Office Holder
♔	Vice President (President of the Senate)	Joseph R. Biden
♕	Speaker of the House	Nancy Pelosi
♖ a1	President Pro Tempore (Senate)	Robert C. Byrd
♖ h1	Senate Majority Leader	Harry Reid
♗ c1	Senate Minority Leader	Mitch McConnell
♗ f1	House Majority Leader	Steny Hoyer
♘ b1	House Republican Leader	John Boehner
♘ g1	House Majority Whip	James E. Clyburn
♙ a2	Texas Senator	John Cornyn
♙ b2	Senate Republican Conference Secretary	Lisa Murkowski
♙ c2	Senate Assistant Minority Leader (Republican Whip)	Jon Kyl
♙ d2	Senate Assistant Majority Leader (Democratic Whip)	Richard Durbin
♙ e2	House Republican Whip	Eric Cantor
♙ f2	Senate Democratic Conference Secretary	Patty Murray
♙ g2	Senate Republican Conference Chair	Lamar Alexander
♙ h2	Texas Senator	Kay Bailey Hutchison

Figure A.10.
Answer key for Figure 3.7.

From *People, Places, Checkmates: Teaching Social Studies with Chess* by Alexey W. Root. Santa Barbara, CA: Libraries Unlimited. Copyright © 2010.

This is one possible answer key for Figure 3.8, with political leaders as of October, 2009.

Symbol	Title	Name of Current Office Holder
♚	President	Barack Obama
♛	Secretary of State	Hillary Rodham Clinton
♜ a8	Secretary of the Treasury	Timothy F. Geithner
♜ h8	Secretary of Defense	Robert M. Gates
♝ c8	Attorney General	Eric H. Holder Jr.
♝ f8	Secretary of the Interior	Kenneth L. Salazar
♞ b8	Secretary of Agriculture	Thomas J. Vilsack
♞ g8	Secretary of Commerce	Gary Locke
♟ a7	Secretary of Veterans Affairs	Eric K. Shinseki
♟ b7	Secretary of Education	Arne Duncan
♟ c7	Secretary of Housing and Urban Development	Shaun L. S. Donovan
♟ d7	Secretary of Health and Human Services	Kathleen Sebelius
♟ e7	Secretary of Labor	Hilda L. Solis
♟ f7	Secretary of Transportation	Raymond L. LaHood
♟ g7	Secretary of Energy	Steven Chu
♟ h7	Secretary of Homeland Security	Janet A. Napolitano

Figure A.11.
Answer key for Figure 3.8.

From *People, Places, Checkmates: Teaching Social Studies with Chess* by Alexey W. Root. Santa Barbara, CA: Libraries Unlimited. Copyright © 2010.

A. In a game I'd played for fun, my opponent began to both sing and tap his feet. I believe it was an effort to annoy me and break my concentration. But out of the concern that it may have been unintentional, I let him continue. B. In order to prevent this you can just tell him to stop. According to Benjamin Franklin you should wait patiently for your opponent to move. I agree with him. However, I think that if the behavior persists to the point of frustration, you should hush them politely.

Jacob wrote:

A. When playing your adversary, ask not of the spectators. Do not help another who is playing a game. This happens often in our class, either by teachers or other students who think they are better than everyone else in the room. B. I think that Ben Franklin would agree and make it to where the technology we have solves the problem. He would probably not know enough, however, to do much about it. I think that all spectators must be behind sound proof walls. Or possibly only allowed to watch on a video to eliminate the problem of spectators' help.

Sam wrote:

A. Giving advice as a spectator. Many people do this during normal games. Saying things like, "I see a good move." B. Ben would ask politely to stop. I think that this problem is mostly up to the offender. Although the players can ask for the spectator to stop, but beyond that there is nothing that the players can do.

Exercise 11. Bughouse does not have an answer key.
Lesson 12. The answers for Figure 4.4 are 1. d. 2. a. 3. g. 4. h. 5. f. 6. e. 7. c. 8. i. 9. b. 10. j.
Exercise 12 does not have an answer key.
Lesson 13 (answer key for Figure 4.8) is 1. True. 2. a. they met new people. 3. c. elementary school students. 4. b. $1,500. 5. d. all of the above. 6. c. 20. Figure A.12 shows factory workers' children in India using a chess set and board donated by Chess Without Borders.

Exercise 13. A simul does not have an answer key. Guidelines for conducting post mortems are in Figure A.13.

Lesson 14. Following are two letters by SMS chess advisory students. I omitted their signatures and home addresses, which are necessary when requesting information. First is a letter by Stephen, sixth grade:

Figure A.12.
Children in India using donated chess equipment.

Dear College Admissions Officer, I would like to join DeVry University because I am a

If the game being analyzed is not your game, you must give three compliments for every one criticism. You should make your comments based on 1–4 below.

For the person whose game is being analyzed, 1–4 also applies to you.

1. Tell if your opening followed the ABCD principles.

2. Tell when you played a good move and why it was good. Usually, good moves for one's side won material, developed pieces, or improved king safety.

3. Tell why you played a poor move and why it was poor. Poor moves for one's side lost material, left pieces undeveloped on the back rank, or put the king in danger.

4. Tell how material was lost or won, such as by a pin, a skewer, a fork, a discovered check, or by having left a chessman en prise.

Figure A.13.
Guidelines for conducting a post mortem.

From *People, Places, Checkmates: Teaching Social Studies with Chess* by Alexey W. Root. Santa Barbara, CA: Libraries Unlimited. Copyright © 2010.

hard-core gamer. I've wanted to make videogames all my life. I hear that with DeVry people graduate years before other colleges. DeVry has some of the highest graduation rates.

Currently I am mostly an A student. I turn my work in on time. People say that I am very creative.

In school I am good at working with groups of people. I think that would come in handy at DeVry. Also, I know what makes a good video game: any game that takes the player on an adventure.

I have accomplished the following (predictions by the end of high school). I was valedictorian. I have taken technology classes, and I have learned programming, some of which are needed to make video games.
I think DeVry should pick me because I have some experience with computers. I think I will be able to make good video games. So if you choose me you won't regret it.

Second, a letter by Zach, eighth grade:

To whom it may concern,

I am currently interested in applying at the University of Florida. I have heard that you have an excellent Aerospace program, granted because you are located near Cape Canaveral.

I am currently making an A average, with high grades in EXPO (Exceptional Potential), Algebra 1, and Science.

I know several facts about various military aircraft, mainly from World War II. I have also been told that I am a highly skilled artist. I am also highly creative.

At the end of high school, I predict that I will be skilled at math, especially in areas such as geometry. I will most likely know much more about aircraft.
You should pick me because I always try my hardest when it is needed. And I am passionate about aircraft.

Exercise 14. White to move and mate in nine. **23. Qh6+ Kxh6 24. Rh1+ Kg5 25. Rdg1+ Kf4 26. Rh4+ Bg4 27. Rgxg4+ Kf3 28. Rg3+ Kxf2 29. Ne4+ Ke1 (or 29....Ke2 30. Bd3+ Ke1 31. Rh1#) 30. Rh1+ Ke2 31. Bd3# 1–0.**

Lesson 15. The answers for Figure 4.14 are A: 3 and 6. B: 2 and 5 C: 1 and 4.

Exercise 15. The answers for Figure 4.15 are 1. d. 2. g. 3. a. 4. c. 5. f. 6. b. 7. e.

Chapter 5

Figure 5.11. Diagram 1 is a checkmate. The black king is in check and cannot take the checking queen, block the check, or move to a safe square. Diagram 2 is a stalemate. The white rook limits all of the black king's moves, and black has no other piece or pawn to move. Yet the black king is not in check. Diagram 3 is a check. The white king can escape the black bishop's check by blocking the check (with Nc3, c3, Bd2, Nbd2, Nfd2, or Qd2) by moving the king to e2. Diagram 4 is a checkmate. The white king is in check and cannot take the checking piece, block the check, or move to a safe square. This particular mate is called the two-rook checkmate.

Appendix B

REFERENCES

References (Annotated)

Along the Silk Road: People, interaction & cultural exchange. (1993). Retrieved from http://www.international.ucla.edu/eas/sum-inst/links/silkunit.htm. Lesson plans and extensive teacher background for teaching the Silk Road, copyright by the Leland Stanford Junior University Board of Trustees.

Ashley, M. (2005). *Chess for success: Using an old game to build new strengths in children and teens*. New York: Broadway Books. Ashley shares stories from competing at chess and from teaching chess, as well as profiling his inner-city students, to show how chess can help at-risk youth.

Benjamin, J. (2007). *American grandmaster: Four decades of chess adventures*. London: Everyman Chess. Benjamin annotates his best games and shares highlights of his career, from chess prodigy to grandmaster to chess teacher and writer.

Chernev, I. (1955). *1000 best short games of chess; A treasury of masterpieces in miniature*. New York: Simon & Schuster. This book contains games of 24 moves or less.

Cohen, S., & Douglass, S. (2006). *Landscape teaching unit 5.2: Afroeurasia and the rise of Islam, 600–1000 CE*. San Diego, CA: San Diego State University and the National Center for History in the Schools (UCLA). Available for download from the Web site http://worldhistory

forusall.sdsu.edu/ as a free.pdf; retrieved from http://worldhistoryfor usall.sdsu.edu/units/five/landscape/05_landscape2.pdf. This teaching unit is part of a model curriculum for teaching middle and high school world history.

Christopher Columbus. (2008). In *Microsoft® Encarta® Online Encyclopedia 2008*. Search for Christopher Columbus at http://encarta.msn.com. Retrieved from http://encarta.msn.com/encyclopedia_761568472/ Christopher_Columbus.html

Curry, J. L. (1994). *Robin Hood and his merry men*. New York: Margaret K. McElderry. Seven Robin Hood stories retold for young readers.

Dynako, B. (2009a, July 16). Chess without borders: Philanthropy on the board. *Chess Life Online*. Retrieved from http://main.uschess.org/ content/view/9524/539. This article tells about money raised through chess tournaments, refreshment sales, and chess book sales to support charitable causes and the establishment of chess clubs in impoverished locations around the world.

Dynako, B. (2009b, October 16). Chess without borders finalist for 2009 Chicago innovation award. *Chess Life Online*. Retrieved from http:// main.uschess.org/content/view/9778/556. This article lists Chess Without Borders as a finalist for an innovative business award.

Eade, J. (2005). *Chess for dummies* (2nd ed.). Hoboken, NJ: Wiley. This book covers the rules of chess, chess history, strategies and tactics, famous games, and tips for tournament and Internet chess play.

Eales, R. G. (1985). *Chess, the history of a game*. New York: Facts on File. This book is a scholarly yet readable history of chess from ancient times until 1980.

Fine, R. (1941). *Basic chess endings*. New York: David McKay. This book is a comprehensive overview of the endgame for intermediate players and higher.

Franklin, B. (1987). The morals of chess. In J.A.L. Lemay (Ed.), *Selections* (pp. 927–931). New York: Viking. (Original work published 1779). To obtain a version of the primary source, with slightly different wording than in Lemay, go to http://www.franklinpapers.org/franklin/ and follow the directions under the heading "searching for words or phrases." Then search for the phrase "Morals of Chess."

GeoQuest: World (Version 1.1) [Computer software]. (2000). Boston: Houghton Mifflin. Interactive maps from different periods of world history. In 2007, my daughter Clarissa used this CD, along with test-preparation guides, to study for the AP World History Exam. She scored a 5, which is the highest possible result.

Gover, B.R. (Ed.). (2006). *Atlas of world geography*. Skokie, IL: Rand McNally. This atlas shows students how to interpret longitude, latitude, symbols, and distances on maps. It also has multiple thematic, political, and physical maps; national flags and questions and answers about countries; and a comprehensive index of cities by longitude and latitude.

Guerber, H. A. (1986). *The Middle Ages*. New York: Avenal. Part of the myths and legends series. One of the legends that William read was Charlemagne's pilgrimage to Jerusalem on pages 177–178.

Kennedy, R. (2008). Tales of the Arabian knights. *Chess Life for Kids*. Kennedy is a columnist for *Chess Life for Kids*. In his columns, available for each of the 2007 and 2008 issues of *Chess Life for Kids*, one character gives hints to another about a chess problem. Although not legends, his columns are examples of interweaving dialogue and chess notation. For issues October of 2008 and after, *Chess Life for Kids* is available as a .pdf download from the USCF Web site http://www.uschess.org/.

Khmelnitsky, I., Khodarkovsky, M., & Zadorozny, M. (2006). *Teaching chess step by step*. Montville, NJ: Kasparov Chess Foundation. Schools may order a complimentary set of three books (1-Teacher's Manual, 2-Exercises Manual, and 3-Activities) by following the instructions at http://www.kasparovchessfoundation.org/.

King, D. (2000). *Chess: From first moves to checkmate*. Boston: Kingfisher. This book features striking artwork and many chess diagrams. King teaches the history and the rules of chess.

Leach, M. (1958). *The rainbow book of American folk tales and legends*. Cleveland, OH: World Publishing. Jared, seventh grade, read about Pecos Bill in this book.

Löhr, R. (2007). *The chess machine* (A. Bell, Trans.). New York: Penguin. (Original work published 2005). Löhr's novel was written in German and is about the Turk, an automaton chess player.

Matthew, D. (1983). *Atlas of medieval Europe*. New York: Facts on File. Written for high school or older readers, this book explains the religious, political, and social influences that shaped medieval Europe.

Matthews, R. (1991). *Explorer*. New York: Knopf. This book is from the Eyewitness Books series. Written for students in grades four to six, *Explorer* has photos and maps of explorations from ancient to modern times.

Neelis, J. (2002). Silk Road trade routes. In *The Silk Road Virtual Art Exhibit*. Retrieved from http://depts.washington.edu/silkroad/exhibit/trade/trade.html. This page is part of The Silk Road Virtual Art Exhibit, http://depts.washington.edu/silkroad/exhibit/index2.html, which has a bibliography of resources, a history of the Silk Road, and interactive map exercises. For example, point to a dot on the map and name the city. Then find out if your guess is correct.

Onuf, K. K. (n.d.). Thomas Jefferson and chess: Documentary sources. In *Monticello, home of Thomas Jefferson*. Retrieved from http://www.monticello.org/reports/quotes/chess.html. This Web site is a resource created by Monticello researchers and respected Jefferson scholars.

Pandolfini, B. (1995). *Chess thinking*. New York: Fireside. This book is a dictionary of chess terms.

Pandolfini, B. (2007). *Treasure chess: Trivia, quotes, puzzles, and lore from the world's oldest game.* New York: Random House. The first chapter covers the rules of chess. Later chapters include quotes about chess from famous people within and outside of the chess world. *Treasure Chess* also has anecdotes and trivia about chess games and chess players.

Philidor, F. D. (1790). *Analysis of the game of chess. By Mr. Philidor. A new edition, improved and greatly enlarged. To which is added, several parties, played by the author blindfold, against three adversaries.* (vol. 2 of 2). London: P. Elmsly. (Original work published, in French, in 1749). Classic text of chess fundamentals written by a world-champion-level player.

Recall of Columbus. (2008). In *U.S. Senate: Art & History Home.* Retrieved from http://senate.gov/artandhistory/art/artifact/Painting_33_00007.htm. When presenting the history of the recall of Columbus, this Web site quotes a Washington Irving paragraph and shows an Augustus Goodyear Heaton painting that hangs in the U.S. Senate.

Root, A. W. (2006). *Children and chess: A guide for educators.* Westport, CT: Teacher Ideas Press. Early chapters give curricular reasons for educators to include chess. The latter part of the book has lesson plans, worksheets, and connections to state standards.

Root, A. W. (2008a, August). Looks at books: A brilliant deception. *Chess Life*, p. 10. This article is my book review of Löhr, R. (2007).

Root, A. W. (2008b). *Science, math, checkmate: 32 chess activities for inquiry and problem solving.* Westport, CT: Teacher Ideas Press. 32 plans organized by chess level and grade level (either 3–5 or 6–8) that teach science, math, or interdisciplinary objectives using chess.

Root, A. W. (2009a, spring). Checkmating advisory and summer boredom. *Tempo, 29*(2), 10–14. This article describes the evolution of SMS advisory (2005–2009), from study halls for all to enrichment advisory options, including chess, for capable students. I also list activities and equipment used at SMS and at MOSAIC.

Root, A. W. (2009b). *Read, write, checkmate: Enrich literacy with chess activities.* Westport, CT: Teacher Ideas Press. In this book, I describe my 2007–2008 middle school literacy project. Also included are the rules and strategies of chess.

Root, A. W., & Wiggins, E. A. (2003). Bughouse for tournament chess players. *Chess Life.* This three-part series appeared in the March, May, and September 2003 issues of *Chess Life.* The articles tell how to pick and treat a bughouse partner and how to play better bughouse openings and tactics. Retrieved from http://www.bughouse.info/academy/essays.html.

Rowland-Warne, L. (1992). *Costume.* New York: Knopf. Part of the Eyewitness Books series, *Costume* is written for ages 9 to 12. It documents clothing from ancient to modern times and includes photos of people wearing recreated period costumes.

Schneider, D. (1994). *Expectations of excellence: Curriculum standards for social studies. Bulletin 89.* Washington, DC: National Council for the Social Studies. Schneider was chair of an 11-person task force for the National Council for the Social Studies (NCSS) to develop these curricular standards. The document is available as a free download from Education Resources Information Center (ERIC). Retrieved from http://www.eric.ed.gov/, search in "ERIC #" for search term ED378131. It is also available for purchase from NCSS, at http://www. socialstudies.org/standards/

Shahade, J. (2007, June 15). Odds and ends. *Chess Life Online.* Retrieved from http://main.uschess.org/content/view/6815/343/. Unlike other Internet sources that incorrectly state that tandem chess uses bughouse rules, Shahade states that tandem chess uses regular chess rules with two-player, nonconsulting teams.

Shahade, J. (2009, May 3). St. Louis psychs up for U.S. champs. *Chess Life Online.* Retrieved from http://main.uschess.org/content/view/9346/343/. This article tells of WGM Jennifer Shahade's simultaneous exhibition in St. Louis on May 2, 2009, which was held to promote the May 7–17, 2009 U.S. Chess Championship.

Shenk, D. (2006). *The immortal game: A history of chess, or how 32 carved pieces on a board illuminated our understanding of war, art, science, and the human brain.* New York: Doubleday. Popular nonfiction title that highlights the origins of chess, famous people who played chess, and ends with how chess is being taught in present-day inner-city classrooms.

Shulman, Y., & Sethi, R. (2007). *Chess! Lessons from a grandmaster.* Rapid City, SD: Spizzirri. Lessons contain either a suggested activity, or a notated and annotated game or game fragment. All lessons are followed by homework problems, usually 10 per lesson. Most pages have two to four diagrams per page. Within the book are 30 black-and-white photos of students playing chess.

Standage, T. (2002). *The Turk: The life and times of the famous eighteenth-century chess-playing machine.* New York: Walker. This book is a nonfiction account of the notorious chess-playing automaton.

Thubron, C. (2007). *Shadow of the Silk Road.* New York: HarperCollins. A travel writer journeys east to west along the Silk Road, beginning in 2003, and documents the people and places en route. He also tells the history or significance of each place visited.

United States Chess Federation, & Kurzdorfer, P. (2003). *The everything chess basics book.* Avon, MA: Adams Media. This book is a comprehensive introduction to the game of chess, similar to Eade (2005).

Van Wijgerden, C. (2008). The step-by-step method. In J. Bosch & S. Giddins (Eds.), *The chess instructor 2009* (pp. 36–53). Alkmaar, The Netherlands: New in Chess. Van Wijgerden's chapter is one of 16 in *The Chess Instructor 2009.* Eleven of the chapters are about training players who already have tournament experience. The remaining five chapters, including Van Wijgerden's, have tips, problems, and insights useful for those working with nontournament players or chess beginners.

Wichary, M. (2006). *Turk* [photograph]. Retrieved from http://www.flickr. com/photos/mwichary/2297118313/. This photo of the Turk chess automaton is available for use under the terms defined here: http:// creativecommons.org/licenses/by/2.0/deed.en

Wolff, P. (2005). *The complete idiot's guide to chess* (3rd ed.). New York: Alpha Books. This book is a comprehensive introduction to the game of chess, similar to Eade (2005).

Yalom, M. (2004). *Birth of the chess queen: A history*. New York: HarperCollins. This book is a scholarly history of chess, which explores whether real-life queens influenced the 1475 rule change that empowered the chess queen.

Photo Credits

Unless otherwise noted in this section, Alexey Root is the photographer for all photos in the book. Other photos were obtained from:

Figure 3.4. Photo taken by Marcin Wichary. Retrieved from http://www. flickr.com/photos/mwichary/2297118313/

This photo is available for use under the terms defined here http:// creativecommons.org/licenses/by/2.0/deed.en

Figure 4.5. This photo of Viswanathan Anand is listed as being in the public domain. Retrieved from http://commons.wikimedia.org/w/index. php?title=File:Viswanathan_Anand_08_14_2005.jpg&oldid=15693629

Figure 4.6. This photo of Judit Polgár at the 1998 U.S. Open was taken by the late Ken Horne. On December 22, 2001, the Chess in Education Certificate Online courses obtained permission from the Nevada Chess Web master to use the photo online and in print publications. As of 2/2/09, this photo is in the photographs section of the Nevada Chess Web site, http://www.nevadachess.org/

Figures 4.8 and A.12. These photos were provided by Dr. Kiran Frey.

The About the Author photo was taken by my daughter Clarissa.

Appendix C

CHESS AT COLLEGES AND UNIVERSITIES

Appendix C and Figure C.1 are based on the research of Amy Michelle Lehman. I was Amy's faculty advisor for her research. She also completed both of my Chess in Education Certificate Online courses. For Appendix C, her work has been edited for brevity. When editing her Figure C.1 in October 2009, I double-checked her URLs, deleted duplicate information, and added descriptions to the right column. Only U.S. institutions have been included.

Web sites such as http://www.chess-class.com/scholarships.html list chess scholarships, but the information is from 2003. Also, some of the listed scholarships are from K–12 schools or from state chess associations. The blog post http://susanpolgar.blogspot.com/2007/04/important-college-chess-information.html listed college chess clubs as of 2007. Some cited in that blog posting are not in Figure C.1.

For Figure C.1, Amy Lehman selected colleges and universities that, now or in the past, either offered scholarships or competed in team chess tournaments. She also focused on four-year, research universities. Figure C.1 includes three community colleges that gave scholarships or fielded chess teams. Scholarship-granting institutions' names are in ***bold italic*** in the left column of Figure C.1. In alphabetical order, higher education Web sites listing chess scholarships as of October 2009 are: Shimer College; Tennessee Technological University; Texas

Tech University; University of Connecticut, School of Engineering; University of Maryland, Baltimore County; The University of Texas at Brownsville and Texas Southmost College; and The University of Texas at Dallas.

As shown in the right column of Figure C.1, higher education chess Web sites usually have:

1. Meetings. Meetings are typically held once a week in a campus building.
2. Mission statements. Sometimes part of a detailed constitution, the mission statement usually states something like: "This club is for playing chess and welcomes all interested students."
3. Advisors and officers. Advisors are faculty members. Officers are students serving as chess club president, secretary, and so forth. Contact information is usually provided for these individuals. If advisors or officers are not listed, but other contact information is provided, then I stated "contact information" in Figure C.1.
4. Tournaments or events or history or links. Some chess Web sites listed tournaments or events, club history (occasionally with photos), or links to other chess Web sites.

Of necessity, in terms of space and fairness, the statements in the right column of Figure C.1 are brief and uniform. Visit the URLs provided to learn about innovative projects such as Princeton's students versus inmates chess match and Yale students volunteering as "America on Board" to teach chess in New Haven schools.

Amy Lehman's Research

Statement of the problem: High school counselors, high school students, and parents cannot easily access college and university chess information. Web sites such as http://www.chess-class.com/scholarships.html provide a comprehensive list of scholarships, but many have not been updated in several years.

Abstract: For my University of Texas at Dallas Undergraduate Research Scholar Award for 2008–2009, I researched higher education chess opportunities in the United States and compiled a database of offerings. That database, after editing by Dr. Root, is in Figure C.1.

Methodology: I began by contacting higher education institutions that, according to Web sites such as http://www.chess-class.com/scholarships.html, had given chess scholarships. Colleges and universities listed as giving scholarships as of 2003 are included in Figure C.1, though not highlighted in bold italic unless chess scholarships are currently featured on their official Web sites. I also queried colleges and universities that have fielded teams for intercollegiate tournaments, such as the Pan American Intercollegiate Team Chess Championship.

In some cases, faculty chess advisors replied via e-mail. Other times I had to do further research to find a contact person. Occasionally I called

School	City	State	School Web Site	Chess Web Site
Amherst College	Amherst	MA	https://www.amherst.edu/	https://www.amherst.edu/campuslife/ studentgroups/chess_club This Web site lists a mission statement and officers.
Arizona State University	Phoenix	AZ	http://www.asu.edu/	http://www.asu.edu/clubs/chess_team/ This Web page lists meetings and officers.
Borough of Manhattan Community College	New York	NY	http://www.bmcc.cuny.edu/	http://www.bmcc.cuny.edu/news/news.jsp?id=399 This news article mentions that BMCC currently has a club team of students, faculty, and staff instead of a championship-winning team as in the 1990s.
Boston College	Chestnut Hill	MA	http://www.bc.edu/	http://www.bc.edu/bc_org/svp/st_org/chess/ This Web page states, "The club no longer exists."
Boston University	Boston	MA	http://www.bu.edu/	http://www.buchess.org This Web site has history, events, and a photo album, but has not been updated since 2007.
Brigham Young University	Rexburg	ID	http://www.byui.edu/	http://www.byui.edu/scroll/archive/20060314/ sports1.html This news article from 2006 mentions an organized tournament on campus.
Brooklyn College	Brooklyn	NY	http://www.brooklyn.cuny.edu/	http://clubscript.brooklyn.cuny.edu/ClubDirectory/ info.php?q=Brooklyn College Chess Club (CLAS) (ACA) This Web page has a mission statement.
Brown University	Providence	RI	http://www.brown.edu/	http://mygroups.brown.edu/Community?action= getOrgHome&orgID=497 http://www.brown.edu/Students/Chess_Club/ These Web pages list meetings.
Bucknell University	Lewisburg	PA	http://www.bucknell.edu/	http://www.orgs.bucknell.edu/chessclub/ This Web site lists meetings, mission statement, advisor, and officers.
Chaminade University	Honolulu	HI	http://www.chaminade.edu/	None found.
City College of New York	New York	NY	http://www1.ccny.cuny.edu/	Listed as one of the campus clubs.
College of New Jersey	Ewing	NJ	http://www.tcnj.edu/	http://www.tcnj.edu/~chessc/ This Web page lists meetings, advisor, and officers, but was last updated in 2007.
Columbia University	New York	NY	http://www.columbia.edu/	http://www.columbia.edu/cu/chess/ This Web site lists meetings, tournaments, and officers, but was last updated in 2008.
Columbus State University	Columbus	GA	http://www.colstate.edu/	None found, but Campus Recreation lists chess as one of its programs.

Figure C.1.
Chess at U.S. higher education institutions.

From *People, Places, Checkmates: Teaching Social Studies with Chess* by Alexey W. Root. Santa Barbara, CA: Libraries Unlimited. Copyright © 2010.

School	City	State	School Web Site	Chess Web Site
Cornell University	Ithaca	NY	http://www.cornell.edu/	http://www.sao.cornell.edu/SO/search. php?igroup=451 This Web page lists meetings, mission statement, advisor, and officers.
Dartmouth College	Hanover	NH	http://www.dartmouth. edu/	http://www.dartmouth.edu/~dchess/ This Web site includes meetings and links.
Del Mar College	Corpus Christi	TX	http://www.delmar.edu/	None found.
Drexel University	Philadelphia	PA	http://www.drexel.edu/	http://www.drexel.edu/news/digest/default. aspx?d=9%2F25%2F2008&id=520 This Web page lists meetings as of fall 2008.
Duke University	Durham	NC	http://www.duke.edu/	http://cgi.duke.edu/web/dukechess/ This Web site has meetings, tournament results, and links.
Eastern Kentucky University	Richmond	KY	http://www.eku.edu/	None found.
Florida Atlantic University	Boca Raton	FL	http://www.fau.edu/	The Boca Raton Chess Club meets at this university; see http://www.bocachess.com/.
Florida State University	Tallahassee	FL	http://www.fsu.edu/	http://www.fsu.edu/~activity/old_websites/TBS/ This Web page lists chess as one of many FSU clubs.
Fordham University	Bronx	NY	http://www.fordham. edu/	Student organizations Web page lists chess as a special interest club.
Georgia Tech	Atlanta	GA	http://www.gatech.edu/	http://cyberbuzz.gatech.edu/chess/ This Web page and the Student organizations Web page list chess club.
Hampshire College	Amherst	MA	http://www.hampshire. edu/	http://chess.hampshire.edu/ This Web site was last updated in 2003.
Harvard University	Cambridge	MA	http://www.harvard. edu/	http://www.hcs.harvard.edu/~hcc/ This Web site lists meetings, officers, photos, and events.
Hawai'i Pacific University	Honolulu	HI	http://www.hpu.edu/	None found.
Indiana University	Bloomington	IN	http://www.indiana. edu/	http://php.indiana.edu/~chess/ This Web site lists meetings, officers, events, and links.
Iowa State University	Ames	IA	http://www.iastate.edu/	http://www.stuorg.iastate.edu/chess/ This Web site was last updated in 2004.
Jackson State University	Jackson	MS	http://www.jsums.edu/	None found.
James Madison University	Harrisonburg	VA	http://www.jmu.edu/	None found.
Kansas State University	Manhattan	KS	http://www.k-state.edu/	http://www.k-state.edu/chessclub/index.html This Web site lists meeting times.
Kenyon College	Gambier	OH	http://www.kenyon.edu/	None found.

Figure C.1.
(continued).

From *People, Places, Checkmates: Teaching Social Studies with Chess* by Alexey W. Root. Santa Barbara, CA: Libraries Unlimited. Copyright © 2010.

School	City	State	School Web Site	Chess Web Site
Lafayette College	Easton	PA	http://www.lafayette.edu/	http://sites.lafayette.edu/stugovt/organization-list/arts-and-culture/ This Web page lists a president.
Massachusetts Institute of Technology	Cambridge	MA	http://www.mit.edu/	http://web.mit.edu/chess-club/www/Chess%20 Club/Welcome%21/Welcome%21.html This Web site has not been updated since 2007.
McNeese State University	Lake Charles	LA	http://www.mcneese.edu/	Chess club is listed as a special interest club, with Dr. Scott Goins <sgoins@mcneese.edu> as advisor.
Miami University	Oxford	OH	http://www.miami.muohio.edu/	http://www.orgs.muohio.edu/chess/PreFAll2009index.html and see also http://main.uschess.org/content/view/9007/500/ The latter page describes how a student restarted a club at Miami University.
Miami Dade College	Miami	FL	http://www.mdc.edu/main/	http://www.mdc.edu/chessteam/ This Web page was last updated in 2004, but http://www.usatoday.com/news/education/2007-03-22-chess-college_N.htm and other newspaper articles highlight the winning chess team.
Mississippi State University	Starkville	MS	http://www.msstate.edu/	http://www.geocities.com/msuchess/index.html This Web site has not been updated since 2001.
Missouri University of Science and Technology	Rolla	MO	http://www.mst.edu/	http://web.mst.edu/~umrchess/ This Web page was updated in 2007.
Montana State University	Bozeman	MT	http://www.montana.edu/	http://www.montana.edu/wwwstuac/clubs.php This Web site lists the University Chess Club, meetings, and its president and advisor.
Morehead State University	Morehead	KY	http://www.moreheadstate.edu/	None found.
New Mexico Tech	Socorro	NM	http://www.nmt.edu/	http://www.nmchess.org/clubs.html According to this state chess association Web site, New Mexico Tech chess club meets once a week.
New York University	New York	NY	http://www.nyu.edu/	http://www.nyu.edu/clubs/chess/ The Web page was last updated in 2006. Provides meetings, and events.
Ohio Wesleyan University	Delaware	OH	http://www.owu.edu/	http://chess.owu.edu/ The Web site lists meetings, officers, advisors, and history.
Oregon State University	Corvallis	OR	http://oregonstate.edu/	http://oregonstate.edu/groups/chess/ The Web site was last updated in 2004.
Penn State	University Park	PA	http://www.psu.edu/	http://clubs.psu.edu/up/chessteam/ The Web site was last updated in 2007.
Porterville College	Porterville	CA	http://www.portervillecollege.edu/	http://www.pc.cc.ca.us/pc_chess/ This Web page lists meetings, advisor, and president.

Figure C.1.
(continued).

School	City	State	School Web Site	Chess Web Site
Princeton University	Princeton	NJ	http://www.princeton.edu/main/	http://www.princeton.edu/~chess/ This Web page was last updated in 2007. Includes information about meetings, events, and tournaments.
Purdue University	West Lafayette	IN	http://www.purdue.edu/	http://www.getinvolved.purdue.edu/Community?action=getOrgHome&orgID=231 This Web page has a mission statement and contact information.
Rhode Island College	Providence	RI	http://www.ric.edu/	http://www.ric.edu/student_activities/sorganizations.php#C This Web page lists meetings, mission statement, president, and advisor.
Roanoke College	Salem	VA	http://roanoke.edu/	http://clubs.roanoke.edu/aainfo/STUDENTLDRROSTER.htm This Web page lists the chess club as inactive.
Rogers State University	Claremore	OK	http://www.rsu.edu/	None found.
Rutgers University	Newark	NJ	http://www.rutgers.edu/	http://www.rci.rutgers.edu/~goeller/index.html This is the Web page of a Rutgers faculty member who also maintains chess Web sites.
St. Mary's University	San Antonio	TX	www.stmarytx.edu	None listed.
San José State University	San José	CA	http://www.sjsu.edu/	http://media.www.thespartandaily.com/media/storage/paper852/news/2008/05/12/News/Chess.Club.Complains.About.Lack.Of.Recognition-3369609.shtml This May 2008 student newspaper article mentions the SJSU chess club.
Shimer College	Chicago	IL	http://www.shimer.edu/	http://www.shimer.edu/admissions/scholarships.cfm Paul Morphy Chess Scholarship Shimer College offers two chess scholarships of up to $2,000 per year each.
Stanford University	Stanford	CA	http://www.stanford.edu/	http://www.stanford.edu/group/chess/ This Web site lists meetings, officers, history, photos, and links.
Stonehill College	Easton	MA	http://www.stonehill.edu/	http://web.stonehill.edu/compsci/Chess_Club/Default.htm This Web page lists meetings, officers, advisor, tournaments and events, and links.
Tennessee Technological University	Cookeville	TN	http://www.tntech.edu/	http://www.tntech.edu/scholarships/chess/ and http://www.tntech.edu/scholarships/cadet-chess-scholarship/ These Web pages lists several scholarships awarded at scholastic chess tournaments, and the name of the chess club advisor.

Figure C.1.
(continued).

From *People, Places, Checkmates: Teaching Social Studies with Chess* by Alexey W. Root. Santa Barbara, CA: Libraries Unlimited. Copyright © 2010.

School	City	State	School Web Site	Chess Web Site
Texas A&M University	College Station	TX	http://www.tamu.edu/	http://studentactivities.tamu.edu/online/organization/OTU5NDQw/profile This Web page lists meetings and mission statement.
Texas A&M University-Commerce	Commerce	TX	http://web.tamu-commerce.edu/	None listed.
Texas A&M University-Kingsville	Kingsville	TX	http://www.tamuk.edu/	http://tamuk.collegiatelink.net/Community?action=getOrgBrowse Use this Web site to (tree) search for chess club, which lists a mission statement.
Texas State University	San Marcos	TX	http://www.txstate.edu/	https://sa.txstate.edu/studentorgs/public/index.asp Use search term *chess* to find mission statement about the chess club, which is listed as active.
Texas Tech University	Lubbock	TX	http://www.ttu.edu/	http://www.depts.ttu.edu/spice/knightraiders/knightraiders.php and http://www.orgs.ttu.edu/knightraiders/ These Web pages list meetings, officers, advisor, history, events, and scholarships.
University of Akron	Akron	OH	http://www.uakron.edu/	Search Activities & Organizations database under Student Life to find a mission statement for the University of Akron Chess Club.
University of California, Berkeley	Berkeley	CA	http://www.berkeley.edu/	http://www.fianchesso.org/ This Web site lists meetings, events, and contact information.
University of Central Oklahoma	Edmond	OK	http://www.uco.edu/	None listed, but advisor for 2008 was Dr. Mark Silcox.
University of Chicago	Chicago	IL	http://www.uchicago.edu/	http://chessclub.uchicago.edu/ This Web site lists meeting times, mission statement, officers, and events.
University of Colorado at Boulder	Boulder	CO	http://www.colorado.edu/	http://castle.colorado.edu/guide/ucsu_club_guide.asp This Web page lists chess club under special interest, and gives meetings, mission statement, and contact information.
University of Connecticut School of Engineering	Storrs	CT	http://www.engr.uconn.edu/	http://www.engr.uconn.edu/chess.php This Web page lists scholarships. http://www.uconnchess.uconn.edu/ This Web page lists meetings, mission statement, and events.
University of Florida	Gainesville	FL	http://www.ufl.edu/	http://www.gatorchessclub.com/ This Web page for the chess club lists meetings, events, officers, advisor, links, and photos.
University of Georgia	Athens	GA	http://www.uga.edu/	http://www.uga.edu/chess/ This Web site has meetings, officers, links, and photos.

Figure C.1.
(continued).

From *People, Places, Checkmates: Teaching Social Studies with Chess* by Alexey W. Root. Santa Barbara, CA: Libraries Unlimited. Copyright © 2010.

School	City	State	School Web Site	Chess Web Site
University of Hawaii at Manoa	Manoa	HI	http://www.uhm.hawaii.edu/	http://www2.hawaii.edu/~uhchess/index.html This Web site has been inactive since 2007.
University of Illinois	Champaign-Urbana	IL	http://illinois.edu/	https://netfiles.uiuc.edu/ro/www/IlliniChessClub/ This Web site lists meetings, tournaments, and president.
University of Iowa	Iowa City	IA	http://www.uiowa.edu/	http://www.uiowa.edu/~chess/ This Web site lists meetings, tournaments, and links.
University of Kentucky	Lexington	KY	http://www.uky.edu/	http://getinvolved.uky.edu/Register/Search/Default.aspx Search this Student Organizations page for chess club, and get a mission statement, president, and advisor.
University of Maryland	College Park	MD	http://www.umd.edu/	http://studentorg.umd.edu/cc/index.html This Web site lists meetings, photos, and links.
University of Maryland, Baltimore County	Baltimore	MD	http://www.umbc.edu/	http://www.umbc.edu/studentlife/orgs/chess/ This Web site lists meetings, advisor, officers, history, photos, links, and scholarships.
University of Massachusetts Amherst	Amherst	MA	http://www.umass.edu/	http://www.umass.edu/rso/chess/ This Web page has meetings, mission statement, president, and tournaments.
University of Memphis	Memphis	TN	http://www.memphis.edu/	http://map.memphis.edu/deptsbldg.php?Building_Id=84&Dept_Id=98 This Web site gives an address for the chess club.
University of Michigan	Ann Arbor	MI	http://www.umich.edu/	http://www.umich.edu/~billiard/clubs/chess.html This Web page lists meetings, mission statement, and a link.
University of Minnesota	Twin Cities	MN	http://www1.umn.edu/	http://www.sua.umn.edu/groups/directory/show.php?id=644 or http://uchessclub.com/ The first Web page lists mission statement and officers. The second Web page lists meetings and a president.
University of Mississippi	Oxford	MS	http://www.olemiss.edu/	http://www.olemiss.edu/orgs/chess/ This Web page has not been updated since 2000.
University of Missouri	Columbia	MO	http://www.missouri.edu/	http://www.students.missouri.edu/~muchess/ This Web site lists meetings, mission statement, advisors, tournaments, and links.
University of Nebraska	Lincoln	NE	http://www.unl.edu/	http://www.unl.edu/chess/ This Web page lists meetings, mission statement, officers, and advisor.
University of New Mexico	Albuquerque	NM	http://www.unm.edu/	http://www4.unm.edu/sac/charter_view.php?id=509 This Web page lists meetings, mission statement, advisor, and officers.

Figure C.1.
(continued).

School	City	State	School Web Site	Chess Web Site
University of North Carolina at Chapel Hill	Chapel Hill	NC	http://www.unc.edu/	http://cf.unc.edu/dsa/union/studorgs/org_details.cfm?ORG_ID=4293 This Web page lists meetings, mission statement, and advisor.
University of North Dakota	Grand Forks	ND	http://www.und.nodak.edu/	http://blizzard.rwic.und.edu/~nordlie/chess/ This Web page was last modified in 2008 and included meetings, president, and links.
University of North Florida	Jacksonville	FL	http://www.unf.edu/	http://www.unf.edu/groups/chess/ This Web page was last modified in 2002. Meetings and advisor listed.
University of North Texas	Denton	TX	http://www.unt.edu/	None listed. Faculty advisor is Dr. Douglas Root <droot@unt.edu>.
University of Oregon	Eugene	OR	http://www.uoregon.edu/	http://gladstone.uoregon.edu/~chess/ This Web site lists meetings, mission statement, officers, links, and photos.
University of Pennsylvania	Philadelphia	PA	http://www.upenn.edu/	http://www.dolphin.upenn.edu/chess/ This Web site lists meetings, mission statement, and links.
University of Pittsburgh	Pittsburgh	PA	http://www.pitt.edu/	http://www.pitt.edu/~schach This Web site was last updated in 2008. It lists meetings, officers, and links.
University of South Dakota	Vermillion	SD	http://www.usd.edu/	http://www.usd.edu/campus-life/student-services/student-organizations/orgDetails.cfm?orgID=43 This Web site lists meetings, mission statement, advisor, and officers.
University of South Florida	Tampa	FL	http://www.usf.edu/	Chess club is listed under student organizations, in the organization directory. The listing gives meetings, mission statement, and contact information.
University of Southern California	Los Angeles	CA	http://www.usc.edu/	http://www-scf.usc.edu/~uscchess/ This Web page lists meetings, mission statement, officers, history, and photos.
University of Tennessee	Knoxville	TN	http://www.tennessee.edu/	None listed.
University of Texas at Brownsville	Brownsville	TX	http://www.utb.edu/	http://blue.utb.edu/sa/chess/ This Web site lists meetings, mission statement, officers, director, history, photos, and links. Scholarship information is at http://blue.utb.edu/sa/chess/scholarships.htm
University of Texas at Dallas	Richardson	TX	http://www.utdallas.edu/	http://chess.utdallas.edu/ This Web site lists meetings, mission statement, officers, director, history, photos, and links. Scholarship information is at http://chess.utdallas.edu/scholarships.html
University of Utah	Salt Lake City	UT	http://www.utah.edu/	http://uofuchessclub.com/ This Web site lists meetings, mission statement, president, advisor, and history.

Figure C.1.
(continued).

School	City	State	School Web Site	Chess Web Site
University of Virginia	Charlottesville	VA	http://www.virginia.edu/	http://scs.student.virginia.edu/~chess/ This Web site lists meetings, officers, and photos, updated in 2008.
Virginia Tech	Blacksburg	VA	http://www.vt.edu/	http://www.chess.org.vt.edu/ This Web site lists meetings, officers, tournaments, and links.
Yale	New Haven	CT	http://www.yale.edu/	http://www.yale.edu/chess/ This Web site lists meetings, mission statement, officers, photos, and events.

Figure C.1.
(continued).

a school's Student Life office to verify what I had previously collected. For schools that gave me the name of a chess contact person, I sent an e-mail requesting information about whether the chess scholarship was still offered, and if so what the scholarship's terms and requirements were. I also investigated chess clubs, teams, and programs.

Conclusion: This type of research is never complete, because many higher education institutions alter, modify, eliminate, or add chess scholarships, clubs, teams, or programs. Chess clubs at featured schools may not maintain Web sites, yet they might still hold meetings. Since my methodology focused on chess scholarship–granting or tournament-participating four-year research institutions, there are likely dozens of active college and university chess clubs not listed here.

Glossary

ABCD opening principles (my acronym; see also Root, 2008b, p. 78):

1. **A**ttack the center;
2. **B**ishops and knights, in either order, should be developed before rooks and queens;
3. **C**astle within the first 10 moves for king safety and to activate the rooks; and
4. **D**elay queen development, so that the queen doesn't become a target.

Adjourned games are postponed, unfinished games. At the adjournment, a diagram is made of the position on the board. In my SMS advisory, the players simply noted whose turn it was to move when play resumed. In a tournament adjournment, one player seals a move in an envelope. That sealed move is opened, and played on the board, when the game resumes. Between adjournment and resumption, players may analyze the game using any resources (computers, friends, books).

Adjudication is "the act of deciding the result of a game without playing it out to a conclusion" (Pandolfini, 1995, p. 22).

Algebraic notation is the most common notation system for writing chess moves. Each square has a name based on its file (a–h) and rank (1–8) coordinates. Short-form algebraic notation, used throughout this book, lists the name of the piece followed by the square it lands on. Long-form algebraic notation lists the starting square and the ending square for each move.

Annotation is commenting on both good moves and mistakes. Depending on the annotator's goals and abilities, annotations give lessons to be learned from (or the truth about) a chess position.

Attack describes "a move or series of moves to mate, gain material, or obtain advantage. It also means to make or threaten such moves" (Pandolfini, 1995, p. 32).

Automaton is a machine or mechanism that is essentially self-operating, such as a robot.

Beginners have 15 hours or less of chess experience. They are still learning the board, rules, and strategies of chess. In terms of USCF rating, they would be approximately 0–200.

Bishop (B) is a chess piece that moves diagonally along unoccupied squares. It can capture an enemy man that is in its path. At the beginning of a game, each player has a light-squared bishop and a dark-squared bishop. A bishop is worth a little more than three pawns (three points), according to most sources.

Blitz chess is played with a clock, set at five minutes per side.

Board is the arena for the chess game and is short for chessboard. The board has 32 light squares and 32 dark squares in an alternating pattern. Squares are arranged in eight vertical columns, called files, and eight horizontal rows, called ranks. When the board is positioned correctly, there is a white square in the lower right corner. For chess teaching, acquire boards with algebraic notation marked on the borders of the board.

Bughouse is a variant of chess. The game is played by two teams of two partners each. One partner plays white and, sitting next to him or her on an adjacent board, the other partner plays black. As captures are made, the partners hand each other captured pieces and pawns. When on move, a player either moves a chess figure already on the board or drops one pawn or piece (previously given to them by their partner) into an unoccupied square. When one person on a team wins, the entire team wins. For all the rules, see http://www.chessvariants.com/multiplayer.dir/tandem.html

Captures occur when a pawn or piece moves to a square occupied by an enemy pawn or piece, except in the case of en passant. The capture removes the enemy piece or pawn from the board. You may not capture your own chessmen. The notation for a capture is a letter x, for example exd5 (meaning the e-pawn takes on d5) or Nxf6 (meaning the knight takes on f6).

Castling (castle) is a move notated 0–0 (kingside castling, "castling short") or 0–0-0 (queenside castling, "castling long"). Castling can be done once per side, per game, if the king and rook that want to castle with each other haven't moved previously and the king is not in check, crossing over a checked square, or ending up on a checked square. Also, there can be no pieces between the king and rook during the castling move. To castle, the king moves two squares toward its rook, and the rook hops over the king and lands on the square horizontally adjacent to the king.

Center of the board includes the squares e4, d4, e5, and d5.

Chatrang, from Persia, is recognizable as an ancestor of chess. It was "a game for two players, played on a board of sixty-four squares" (Eales, 1985, p. 26).

Chaturanga, a term that also referred to the four limbs of an army, "foot-soldiers, cavalry, chariots and elephants" (Eales, 1985, p. 31). It is a game from India, circa 450. It is a precursor to chatrang.

Check (+) is a direct attack on a king by an enemy piece or pawn. The king must get out of check by capturing the checking piece or pawn, blocking the check with one of his own men, or moving to a square that is not attacked.

Checkmate (++ or # or mate) is when the king is in check and cannot escape from check. Being checkmated means that player has lost the chess game.

Chess in Education Certificate Online courses have been offered by The University of Texas at Dallas since the fall of 2001. The courses are available nationally, via the Internet. For course information, search for "Chess in Education Certificate" at the UT TeleCampus: http://www.telecampus.utsystem.edu/

Chessmen are the "pieces and pawns considered as a group" (Pandolfini, 1995, p. 66).

Clocks are used to time chess games. One's time runs when it is one's move. At the completion of one's move, one punches a button to start one's opponent's clock running. Some games use sudden death (SD) time controls. That is, one must finish one's whole game before the time elapses. Common SD time controls include G/5 (game in 5 minutes per player, called blitz or speed chess) and G/30 (game in 30 minutes per player, called action chess). G/30 is the fastest time control allowed for a game to be rated under the regular rating system by USCF; G/5–G/29 are rated under a separate quick chess rating system.

In contrast, some tournaments use traditional time controls such as 40/2, 20/1, 20/1: make 40 moves before your first 2 hours elapse, then make 20 moves per hour for the next two time controls. For both SD and traditional time controls, a loss on time (a flag fall) means a loss of the game, except when the side "winning on time" does not have sufficient material to deliver a checkmate (e.g., only has a K and B, or only has a K and an N; see *draw*).

Defense is "a move or series of moves designed to meet opposing threats and attacks, whether immediate or long range. In the openings, a defense is a system of play whose characteristic positions are determined largely by Black" (Pandolfini, 1995, p. 88).

Demonstration board (demo board) is a large, upright chess board that either hangs from a nail or map hook or is mounted on an easel. Its chessmen are held on magnetically or fit into slots. The demonstration board is used for showing chess moves to groups of students. One can order demonstration boards from most chess retailers, including USCF.

Descriptive notation is an older system of notation than algebraic notation. Descriptive notation is based on the names and squares that pieces occupy at the beginning of the game, for example, 1. Kt.-KB3 (or the Kt. to its K. B. third square) means knight to king's bishop's three. In short-form algebraic, that same move would be written 1. Nf3. In long-form algebraic, it would be 1. Ng1-f3 or 1. g1-f3.

Developing pieces properly in the opening involves moving them from their starting squares to squares that attack the center of the board or other important targets.

Diagonal is "a slanted row of same-colored squares. There are 26 different diagonals on the chessboard" (Pandolfini, 1995, p. 90).

Diagram is a two-dimensional representation of a chess position. Traditionally, the white chessmen start at the bottom of a chess diagram. One can make diagrams by hand, by abbreviating the chessmen's names (K, Q, R, B, N, and P) and circling the black chessmen. Or one can use a software program such as ChessBase Light, available from http://www.chessbase.com/download/index.asp, which includes fonts that give figurine representations of white and black pieces.

Discovered check is "the movement of a piece or pawn that results in a check by an unmoved piece" (Eade, 2005, p. 320).

Draws are scored as a half a point for each player. As Eade (2005, p. 321) wrote, there are several ways for a draw to result: "(a) by agreement of both players, (b) by stalemate, (c) by the declaration and proof of one player that the same position has appeared three times (with the same player to move), (d) by the declaration and proof of one player that there have been 50 moves during which no piece [or pawn] has been taken and no pawns have been moved, although there are some exceptions to the 50 move rule." If one's opponent runs out of time (see *clock*)—but one doesn't have sufficient material to checkmate—a draw is declared. Finally, in some cases, tournament directors may adjudicate games as draws, wins, or losses, usually when there is a time constraint to complete a club game or a team match.

En passant (e.p.) is French for in passing and is pronounced ahn pah-SAHNT. The en passant capture can be executed by pawns that are on one's own fifth rank. On an algebraically labeled board, the fifth rank for a black pawn is rank 4. When an enemy pawn does a double jump to the square adjacent to the fifth-rank pawn, then that pawn can capture the enemy pawn as if it had only moved one square. The en passant capture is optional. If chosen, en passant is played on the half-move immediately following the enemy pawn's double jump.

En prise is a French term meaning "in take," and is pronounced ahn PREEZ. Putting a chessman en prise means to move it to, or to fail to remove it from, a square where it can be captured for free.

Endgame (ending) is the stage of the game that occurs after approximately 15 points in pieces (not pawns) have been exchanged for each side (Fine, 1941, p. 441). That is, if each side has traded off a queen and two minor pieces, then usually the position is classified as an endgame. Often the king becomes active in the endgame, attacking enemy pawns and supporting the promotion of his own pawns.

Fédération Internationale des Échecs (FIDE), Web site http://www.fide.com, is the world chess federation, with 161 countries (including the United States, represented by USCF) as members. FIDE maintains a rating system and awards international titles such as Grandmaster (GM), International Master (IM), and Fide Master (FM). FIDE also organizes world championships.

Fianchetto is an Italian word meaning "little flank" (Wolff, 2005, p. 169). It is pronounced fee-an-KET-toe. Fianchettoed bishops on b2 or g2 for white and b7 or g7 for black attack the center squares along the longest diagonals.

FIDE Master (FM) title can be earned by achieving a FIDE rating of over 2300 at some point in time.

Files are the vertical columns of squares on the board. There are eight files, labeled a, b, c, d, e, f, g, and h.

Forks are simultaneous attacks on two or more chess pawns or pieces.

Grandmaster (GM) is an international title awarded by FIDE to players who perform above a predetermined level (2600 FIDE) at tournaments with other titled players. Usually it takes three such performances (three norms) to get the GM title.

Illegal move is one prohibited by the rules of chess. When noticed before the end of the game, it causes the position to be reset to just before the illegal move. At that point, a legal move must be played instead.

Intermediate scholastic chess players have 15 or more hours of chess instruction or playing experience. They already know the board, the rules, and some basic strategies of chess. They may already know how to read and write chess games. Their USCF rating or playing strength would be approximately 200–900.

International Master (IM) is a title awarded by FIDE to players who perform above a predetermined level (2451 FIDE) at tournaments with other titled players. Usually it takes three such performances (three norms) to get the IM title.

J'adoube is pronounced juh-DOOB and is a French term meaning "I adjust." One says j'adoube before straightening a chessman. If one fails to say j'adoube (or I adjust), then the touch move rule states that the touched chessman must be moved.

Kibitzing is to comment on chess moves, either during a game in progress or during a post mortem, within the hearing of the players and without their permission.

King (K) is able to move one square in any direction. The king captures the same way that it moves. When the king is checkmated or stalemated, the game is over. See also *castling*.

Kingside is the half of the board that includes the e-, f-, g-, and h-files.

Knight (N) is the piece that looks like a horse. Like a horse, it can jump over pieces and pawns. The knight's move is in the shape of capital L. Or the knight's move can be described as two squares horizontally followed by one square vertically, or two squares vertically followed by one square horizontally. It captures an enemy chessman by landing on the square of that chessman. The knight is generally said to be worth three pawns (three points).

Ladder games are played at the pace of one game against one opponent per meeting session. Winning a game may move a player onto the ladder or higher up on the ladder.

Luft is a German word meaning air. Moving a pawn in front of a castled king, to avoid being back-rank mated, creates an escape square or luft for that king.

Masters possess a USCF rating between 2200 and 2400. Ratings above 2400 are senior masters or are referred to by their FIDE titles.

Material refers to captured chessmen. If you have captured more points than your opponent, then you are material ahead.

Middlegame is the phase between the opening and the endgame. While specific openings and endings may be memorized, middlegames feature long-term strategies and calculations of tactics.

Mobility is the ability to move to different parts of the board. One can talk about the mobility of particular pieces and pawns in different positions. For example, a bishop has more mobility than a knight when there are lots of open diagonals, but a knight may have more mobility than a bishop if diagonals are blocked by pawn chains.

Moves in chess refer to either making a move for one side, or to the combined white and black move pair. Thus when a chess problem reads, "White to move," it is white's turn. But when the problem states, "White checkmates in three moves," that means three white moves (with the required black moves also played); in other words, a white move and black move, a second white move and black move, and a third white move completing the mate.

Olympiad is a FIDE-organized tournament "held every two years in which teams from FIDE member countries compete. The first Chess Olympiad was held in London in 1927" (Eade, 2005, p. 331).

Opening refers to the first 10 or so moves of a chess game, during which time players develop most or all of their pieces. The opening is followed by the **middlegame,** which is followed by the endgame.

Pawns (P) are the smallest units on the chessboard. They move forward but capture diagonally. A pawn may move one or two squares on its initial move. When it reaches its eighth rank, it is promoted. See also *promoting* and *en passant*. A pawn is worth one point.

Perpetual check is when one side may check the other side's king continually and the checked side is unable to stop the checks. The game is either a draw by agreement or as a case of the threefold repetition of position rule. See also *draw*.

Pieces are not pawns but are kings, queens, rooks, bishops, and knights.

Pins immobilize lower-value pawns or pieces, because those chessmen must shield a higher-value piece from an enemy queen, rook, or bishop. The lower-value pawn or piece is pinned if, when it moves, the higher-value piece could be captured by the enemy. For example, a white bishop could pin a black knight to a black queen. If the knight moved off the bishop's diagonal, the white bishop could take the black queen. The previous example is a relative pin, because the knight could legally move. An absolute pin occurs when the higher-value piece is the king. In that case the pinned piece cannot legally move, as moving would expose the king to check.

Points are a guide for the fair exchange of pieces. That is, just as one would not want to trade $9 for $3, one would likewise usually refuse to trade a Q (9 points) for a N (3 points). The other point values are: P (1 point), B (3 points), and R (5 points). A value is not placed on the king, since he cannot be traded, but his power is between 3 and 4 points. Points can also refer to a player's score in a tournament; for example, "He has one point" means that he either won one game or drew two games. Points can also refer to chess rating, as in "Alexey Root's June 2008 USCF rating was 2006, which is more than 250 points below her peak rating of 2262."

Position is the arrangement of the pieces and pawns on the board.

Post mortem is conducted after a chess game is completed. The participants in the game discuss their moves, sometimes joined by interested observers.

Problem is a chess position, usually represented on a diagram, for which there is a specific solution. For example, a problem might state, "White to move and mate in three." The person studying the problem would either set up the diagrammed position on a chess board to figure out the three moves, or solve the problem mentally.

Promoting or Promotion is when a pawn reaches its eighth rank and is converted to a N, B, R, or Q. One usually queens a pawn, as a queen is the piece worth the most points. Promoting to any piece except the queen is called under-promoting or under-promotion.

Queen is worth about nine pawns (nine points), according to most sources. On any given move, she can choose to move like a rook or like a bishop.

Queenside is the half of the board that includes the d-, c-, b-, and a-files.

Ranks are the horizontal rows of squares on a board. There are eight ranks, labeled 1, 2, 3, 4, 5, 6, 7, and 8 in algebraic notation.

Rating is a number assigned to a player based on his or her performance against other rated players. USCF ratings range from the low 100s to around 2800. More about ratings is at http://www.renaissancek nights.org/IL%20Scholastic/Handouts/Handouts%20PDFs/EloRat ingSystem.pdf.

Rook (R) is a chess piece that moves horizontally and vertically, as many squares as are not blocked by chessmen of its own color. It can capture an enemy piece or pawn that is in its path. The rook is usually said to be worth five pawns (five points). See also *castling*.

Sacrifice means "to deliberately give up material to achieve an advantage," such as a checkmating attack against the enemy king (Eade, 2005, p. 335).

Score sheet contains the notation for a chess game, as written by one of that game's participants.

Set of chessmen is the combined collection of 16 pawns, four rooks, four knights, four bishops, two queens, and two kings. Half of the set are black pieces and pawns; half are white.

Shatranj is the Arabic name for Persian chatrang. Because of the Qur'an's prohibition against images, "Muslim craftsmen abstracted the explicit Persian figures into elegant, hand-carved, cylindrical or rectangular stones with subtle indentations, bumps, and curves to symbolize a throne or a tusk or a horse's head" (Shenk, 2006, p. 33).

Simultaneous exhibition (or "simul" for short) is when a single strong chess player plays several people all at the same time. "Numerous boards are set up, in a circle or rectangle, and the single player stands inside this area, moving from board to board, usually playing a single move at a time" (Eade, 2005, p. 336).

Skewers and pins are tactics directed toward two enemy pieces on the same line (diagonal, rank, or file). In a skewer, the high-value piece is first along the line of attack. When it moves off the line, the newly exposed piece of lesser value can be captured.

Stalemate is when a king is not in check but there are no legal moves for his side. It is scored as a draw.

Staunton chess sets are required at FIDE tournaments. Created by Nathaniel Cook in 1835, the design is named after the great English player Howard Staunton (Eade, 2005, p. 337).

Tactics are moves that force short-term sequences to win material or another advantage. Some common tactics are pins and forks.

Tandem chess is usually played with a clock (set at five minutes per side), with two players on each team alternating moves. There is just one chess board for the four participants. Partners may not talk to each other.

Touch move rule states that if players touch a particular pawn or piece then they have to move it. If they touch an opponent's pawn or piece, then they must capture it. Once they remove their hand from a chessman, the move is completed and cannot be changed. If a legal move is impossible with the touched pawn or piece, another move must be selected. If a chessman simply needs to be straightened, say "I adjust" (or the French term *J'adoube*) and then replace the pawn or piece on its square without penalty.

Tournaments are chess contests for more than two players.

Trade is to exchange your pawn or piece for your opponent's.

United States Chess Federation (USCF) has a main Web site (http://www.uschess.org) and a sales Web site (http://www.uscfsales.com/). The USCF is the official governing body for chess in the United States. It also runs the USCF rating system, which ranks member players. USCF produces two magazines: *Chess Life*'s instructional articles are at the intermediate level and higher; *Chess Life for Kids* provides intermediate-level articles for children 12 and under.

Variations are alternatives to the moves that were actually played in the game under analysis. Variations are also "any sequence of moves united by a logical, purposeful idea, either played in a game or proposed by an analyst. Also a specific opening line, such as the Dragon Variation of the Sicilian Defense" (Pandolfini, 1995, p. 261).

Wins in chess occur when one player checkmates the other player, or when that player's opponent resigns or loses on time (see *clock*). A win is scored as one point for the winning player on the tournament wall chart.

Woman FIDE master (WFM) is a title awarded for achieving a FIDE rating of 2100 or higher. It is less prestigious than the Woman International Master or Woman Grandmaster titles.

Woman Grandmaster (WGM) is a title awarded by FIDE to players who perform above a predetermined level (2401 FIDE) at tournaments with other titled players. Usually it takes three such performances (three norms) to get the WGM title. A Woman Grandmaster title is almost as prestigious as an International Master title (a title not restricted by gender).

Zugzwang is a German word, pronounced TSOOKS-vahng, designating a situation in which to move is to lose. When in zugzwang, every move one might play worsens one's position.

Zwischenzug is German, pronounced TSVEYE-shun-tsook, and literally means "intermediate move." In English, it is sometimes called an "in-between move." Pandolfini (1995, p. 272) wrote, "It's usually a way to gain advantage by inserting a surprise finesse before following through on an obvious response, such as a recapture."

Index

About the Author

ALEXEY W. ROOT has a PhD in education from the University of California, Los Angeles. She is a senior lecturer in the School of Interdisciplinary Studies at The University of Texas at Dallas (UTD). She has taught UTD education classes, tutored prospective teachers for certification exams, and supervised student teachers. She served as the associate director of the UTD Chess Program. Root currently teaches UTD's Chess in Education Certificate Online courses, available worldwide for college credit via the UT TeleCampus platform (http://www.uttc.org). Root has been a tournament chess player since she was nine years old. Her most notable chess accomplishment was winning the U.S. Women's championship in 1989. She lives in Denton, Texas, with her husband Doug, children Clarissa and William, and rabbit Abba.

Contact Dr. Root at alexey.root@gmail.com.